Solidarity & Care

ALANA LEE GLASER

Solidarity & Care
Domestic Worker Activism in New York City

TEMPLE UNIVERSITY PRESS
Philadelphia • *Rome* • *Tokyo*

DWU

**Domestic Workers
United**

All royalties from the sale of this book go to Domestic Workers United.

TEMPLE UNIVERSITY PRESS
Philadelphia, Pennsylvania 19122
tupress.temple.edu

Library of Congress Cataloging-in-Publication Data

Names: Glaser, Alana L., author.
Title: Solidarity & care : domestic worker activism in New York City /
Alana Lee Glaser.
Other titles: Solidarity and care
Description: Philadelphia : Temple University Press, 2023. | Includes
bibliographical references and index. | Summary: "This ethnographic book
chronicles the impact of the 2010 New York Domestic Workers' Bill of
Rights on the multicultural, immigrant-led organizations responsible for
its passage as well as its unexpected sequelae in the daily lives of
individual Latina, Caribbean, and West African women working as
caregivers in New York City"— Provided by publisher.
Identifiers: LCCN 2022060140 (print) | LCCN 2022060141 (ebook) | ISBN
9781439922453 (cloth) | ISBN 9781439922460 (paperback) | ISBN
9781439922477 (pdf)
Subjects: LCSH: Domestic Workers United. | Women household employees—New
York (State)—New York—Social conditions. | Women household
employees—New York (State)—New York—Interviews. | Women household
employees—Political activity—New York (State)—New York. | Women
foreign workers—New York (State)—New York—Social conditions. | Women
foreign workers—New York (State)—New York—Interviews. | Women foreign
workers—Political activity—New York (State)—New York. | Household
employees—Legal status, laws, etc.—New York (State)—New York. |
Foreign workers—Legal status, laws, etc.—New York (State)—New York.
Classification: LCC HD8039.D52 G319 2023 (print) | LCC HD8039.D52 (ebook)
| DDC 647².2082097471—dc23/eng/20230414
LC record available at https://lccn.loc.gov/2022060140
LC ebook record available at https://lccn.loc.gov/2022060141

Contents

Preface

On a warm July Saturday, I entered the recreational room of a Brooklyn church shortly after three o'clock in the afternoon.* The monthly membership meeting of Domestic Workers United (DWU) was nearly ready to begin. The church's large white-walled and hardwood-floored auditorium shone with a green glow from the DWU T-shirts that were on display, arranged by size and language—half in Spanish and half in English. As usual, Jane, a longtime DWU member, welcomed me to the meeting, directing me to a nearby table stocked with multilingual meeting agendas, informational handouts, and folders for newcomers. Between the translation-equipment table—where members could check out individual receivers to facilitate real-time translation from English to Spanish—and the dues table that I occasionally helped run, small groups of women congregated and greeted one another.

A small cohort of DWU members, all Caribbean women between forty and sixty years old, gathered near the church entrance, reacting to an employment advertisement. The job posting advertised for a live-in nanny/housekeeper to care for four children, ages unspecified. The small group laughed at the posting's detailed description of extensive housekeeping duties, as Jane handed me the advertisement. "You have to read this," she implored.

A bit later, Katherine, a published poet, musician, and full-time nanny recited the job description as a poem, performing it for the thirty mostly middle-aged members gathered during the cultural component of the meeting. As one of the stewards of DWU's cultural committee, Katherine was well known for her impromptu performances, many of which reinterpreted job postings and employer instructions to dramatic and humorous effect. She delivered each line of the employment advertisement in melodic, Trinidadian-accented speech, transforming the makeshift meeting hall into an improvised open-mic stage. Reading from the employer's instructions, she intoned, "Before you go out for the night please be sure the kitchen eating area is clean, dishes cleaned, and kitchen counters." Looking up at her secular congregation, she remarked incredulously, "And the four children haven't been mentioned yet!"

Groans and laughs of agreement reverberated throughout the space. She invited us to join her after each cleaning task description with the chorus "and the four children haven't been mentioned yet." With this refrain, Katherine repeatedly drew our attention to the linguistic negative space of the posting, reminding us—the audience—of the priorities represented, and those omitted, in the advertisement. She implicitly evaluated the author, too, by mocking the detailed cleaning instructions absent any description of the childcare responsibilities associated with the job. And she authorized us to join in her evaluation.

Katherine composed herself and resumed her recitation: "On mornings you should do a very thorough dusting." In an aside, she noted, "If the four children ever come home," trailing off into inaudible but shared grumbling. *There is no way to care for four children while doing all of this housework.* Katherine's refrain commented disapprovingly on the lack of attention to the children, while also engendering a communal condemnation of the material excesses represented in the intricate cleaning instructions. With feigned earnestness, Katherine resumed reading: "The kitchen should be kept clean, but one to two times a week should be thoroughly cleaned. The hallway should be cleaned . . . as needed." She paused again after she read the next three words—"The fridge upstairs"—shaking her head with a deep, generous chuckle.

Her laughter—implying amusement at the extravagance of two refrigerators in one household—began in her throat but moved to her gut, becoming breathless, as she again bent forward to collect herself before circling her impromptu stage to compelling theatrical effect. Beginning once again: "The fridge upstairs and downstairs should be cleaned out once a week," she proclaimed with a burst of laughter, "with the food thrown out and the shelves and bins cleaned out." She looked up. Now we were all in on the joke. Experiencing the co-construction of this narrative poem, the room hummed with a giddy rumbling, as these diverse domestic workers crafted their collective judgment of the employer, affirming their shared experiences: *We've all worked for this type of person before.*

Returning to her refrain, "and the four children haven't been mentioned yet," Katherine raised her left hand as though she was directing a symphony. The crowd followed her direction, singing the lines that had come to represent both an inside joke and a condemnation of this anonymous but all-too-representative employer. Katherine punctuated the phrase with a wave of her hand, taking a moment to allow the laughter to settle before beginning her closing stanza. "Before the end of the week, all the laundry should be done," she laughed. With perfect timing and crescendo, the audience burst into "and the four children haven't been mentioned yet!" before devolving into applause and laughter, as Katherine accepted her praise with a gentle bow.

Katherine's performance, along with her audience's participation in it, demonstrates how DWU members use performance, storytelling, and shared grievances to overcome the isolation of working for individual families in private homes. By communally sharing workplace complaints at DWU meetings, nannies—often working on their own in private homes—commiserate with and support one another. These collective performances of complaint are a critical source of solidarity and power for nannies. They also illustrate, and poke fun at, some of the daily indignities that domestic workers encounter in their positions. Katherine's humorous interpretation—accompanied by a lively embodied performance of disbelief, disapproval, and bemusement—exaggerated domestic workers' daily evaluations and judgments of their employers. In repeating the chorus back to her, as Katherine instructed us to do, we affirmed her dissatisfaction with the overwhelming attention to cleaning in the advertisement. Through this shared sense of indignation, nannies' collective judgments are transformed from singular speech events into something that is communally experienced.

Such performances and storytelling transform care workers' individual frustrations into communal political acts, providing camaraderie and motivation to the women who do this work and sustaining their struggles to improve their working conditions. For nannies, housekeepers, and home health workers, who are isolated in their employers' homes, the communal setting of DWU meetings offers the opportunity to collectively experience, express, and object not only to their specific working conditions but also to the broader global processes that facilitate them. Through these collective complaints, domestic workers share their experiences and strategies for navigation and resistance with one another. Otherwise, domestic workers' workplace issues might remain hidden in the isolated homes where they work. Performances like Katherine's as well as less dramatic but useful conversations at meetings and events provide a sense of solidarity and shared struggle for DWU members.

The DWU meeting at which Katherine improvised her performance remains memorable not only for Katherine's charismatic command of the room but also for the spirit of solidarity and unity that characterized the afternoon. I have described this scene many times in the course of my research on care-worker activists, often exhibiting the same exuberance and giddiness in retelling that I experienced as an audience member that Saturday afternoon. I share it now at the beginning of this book about Domestic Workers United to provide a sense of how incisive DWU activists' critiques are and how enjoyable DWU meetings can be, as they provide the occasion for DWU members to collectively analyze their working conditions. As we will see through comparison with the experiences and perceptions of care workers who are not affiliated with DWU or any collective advocacy organization, DWU's transformative solidarity has the potential to improve the circumstances of individual workers, even as the group remains primarily focused on addressing structural issues that shape domestic work in the United States.

Despite the isolation of domestic work, and its historical exclusion from U.S. labor laws, DWU and its allies have successfully fought for new laws that protect domestic workers in the private homes where

they work. This book describes DWU's activism and domestic workers' solidarity, in their dual goal of improving their working conditions and supporting one another, at a time of worsening employment
conditions for many people around the world. As we will see, DWU's
solidarity provides a blueprint for workers across neoliberal industries to advocate for themselves and one another.

---

*Portions of the Preface previously appeared in Alana Glaser, "Collective Complaint:
New York City Care Workers' Community, Performance, and the Limits of Labor
Law," *PoLAR: Political and Legal Anthropology Review* 43, no. 2 (2020): 195–210.
https://doi.org/10.1111/plar.12377.

Acknowledgements

I am indebted to Domestic Workers United members and staff for the warmth and wisdom they shared with me, and for their fight to bring change to domestic work and to the entire working class. I am so thankful to the many women, families, activists, and workers in New York City who shared their time, expertise, and experiences with me. To protect their privacy, I do not mention them by name. But knowing each of them has enriched my life beyond this project, and I hope my gratitude to them is reflected in this ethnography. I am especially grateful to the members and staff of Jews for Racial and Economic Justice, the Malian Cultural Center, the Ivorian Congregation of the Bronx, and the National Domestic Workers Alliance for their openness and for allowing me to be a part of their communities for a short time. The women and families with whom I worked extended care and love to me during my fieldwork, and their support for me—as a friend, comrade, and student—only hints at the full range of their professional caregiving labor.

The Wenner-Gren Foundation funded the research on which this project is based. I am grateful to Northwestern University's Department of Anthropology, Graduate School, African Studies Program, Buffet Center, and Dispute Resolution Research Center of the Kellogg School of Management for their institutional support and generous funding. I am also grateful to St. John's University for research funds that supported the writing of this manuscript. Some of the ethnographic data presented here also appear in a chapter I wrote for Victoria Haskins and Claire Lowrie's anthology *Colonization and Domestic Service: Historical and Contemporary Perspectives* (Routledge USA, 2014), which grew out of a symposium they convened. I am indebted to them for organizing that collection and bringing together such an inspiring group of scholars researching domestic labor.

At Northwestern University, Micaela di Leonardo cultivated a community of scholars working in the culture and political-economy tradition, broadening my intellectual and political horizons. Her scholarly example and instruction encouraged me to pursue fieldwork on workers in the United States. D. Soyini Madison shaped my academic path a decade before I began research, inspiring me and introducing me to ethnography, social justice performance, and the International Monetary Fund's debt repayment policies. Robert Launay's guidance and theoretical expertise supported my training as an ethnographer and a broadly engaged anthropologist. Shalini Shankar's insights, both cultural and linguistic, have challenged me to sharpen my arguments. Jane Collins's expertise in U.S. labor and economy has been instrumental to my analysis. I also benefited from working closely with Karen Tranberg Hansen and Katherine Hoffman, and from the guidance of Helen Swartzman and Ana Aparicio. I am also grateful to my earlier mentors: Jan Paris, Charles Kurzman, Maria DeGuzman, Robin Nagle, Robert Dimit, Lok Siu, Heather Lukes, and Sofia Shwayri.

This book would not have been possible without the support of Shaun Vigil at Temple University Press. Ana Croegaert and Adrienne Pine have been generous mentors and friends over the course of my writing. I am indebted to Erin Martineau for her incredible editing acumen, which has improved this manuscript significantly. I also thank Barrie Zipkin for editing an early chapter. I have benefitted immensely from conversations on the dynamics of reproductive labor over the past few years with Julietta Hua, Cati Coe, Swapna Banerjee, Victoria Haskins, and Claire Lowrie. I am grateful to Faith Kares, Dafna Strauss, Lauren Adrover, Brooke Bocast, Karima Borni, Elizabeth Hartman, Almita Miranda, and Dario Valles for their collaboration and critique and, especially, to Heather Silvestri for years of guidance and friendship. I am incredibly fortunate to have had a career full of wonderful colleagues, now at St. John's University and previously at National Nurses United.

I cannot adequately thank my family members, too numerous to mention by name, for all of their love and support. Thank you to my parents, my brother, and, especially, Matthew Zipkin, my XVIIII, XVIII, and XVII, for his support and care—and to Christian for teaching us to care so completely.

Solidarity & Care

Introduction

I stood behind a long folding table in the rear of a cavernous Lower Manhattan union meeting hall, arranging a cheese plate, as the crowd began to enter for the Domestic Workers United (DWU) tenth anniversary gala. Early attendees—overwhelmingly middle-aged, Caribbean women—entered in groups, dressed in elegant suits made from metallic fabrics in purple, green, and pink, and in sharp business attire in solemn browns and blues. Women with intricate updos and sparkling jewelry congregated near the entryway and joined friends already seated at round tables. Groups of women danced between the crowded tables to live reggae performed by a DWU member and her band.

By the time the program began, the hall was standing room only. Priscilla Gonzalez, then director of DWU—the history-making New York City advocacy organization of "Caribbean, Latina, and African nannies, housekeepers, and elderly caregivers"—welcomed the crowd, thanking attendees for their support. Gonzalez recalled attending a similar meeting with her mother, a New York City domestic worker, in that same union hall seven years earlier at one of the first domestic worker conventions. These words were echoed in her eloquent statement in the program booklet: "When I first became involved with DWU, I knew I had found something special. It was a place where my

mother's profession as a domestic worker was finally seen as dignified and worthy of respect," she wrote in the gala's program booklet.
The passage continued: "For us, DWU represented hope for a better
tomorrow. Immigrant women of color were leading a movement to
transform the domestic work industry and bring meaningful change
to the entire working class." Gonzalez's words drew together many of
the significant implications of domestic worker solidarity in the lives
of care workers who had fought for dignity and respect in their own
workplaces and for the entire working class.

I had begun conducting research in New York City earlier that
year, in the summer of 2010, just as DWU celebrated the passing of
the New York State Domestic Workers' Bill of Rights, the first-ever
U.S. legislation protecting home-based workers. The gala, held in November, coincided with the implementation of the Domestic Workers'
Bill of Rights, commemorating both the hard-won legislative victory
and the decade of demonstrating, lobbying, and organizing by the
hundreds of domestic workers, religious communities, supportive
union members, legislators, and activist employers who facilitated it.

The passage of the Domestic Workers' Bill of Rights is the background against which this ethnography is set. It represents a significant and historic change to U.S. labor law and to the lives of workers
and activists who made its passage possible. Yet, the actual focus of
this book—and its message, in so far as it has one—is not about the
passage of a law per se, although that is an accomplishment worthy of
praise and attention. Rather, this book is about how domestic workers organized against precarity, isolation, and exploitation in a deeply
personal field. What motivated their activism? How did they identify
and recruit one another to their cause? How have domestic workers
used storytelling to build camaraderie and solidarity? What might
political education look like for this group of women workers? What
has solidarity entailed—both before and after the passage of this legislation that they envisioned together, more than two decades ago? How
did DWU's solidarity activism shape their members' work experiences
and analyses, as compared with domestic workers who are not a part
of a collective organization like DWU?

Solidarity & Care is about how women working as housekeepers,
childcare providers, and home health aides joined together to support
one another and improve their working conditions through protests,

Figure I.1 DWU's director speaks about the power of domestic worker solidarity.

lobbying, and performance. Foregrounding the political organizing of informal workers—those outside of formal labor law protections—*Solidarity & Care* also illustrates the ongoing impact of exploitation, racism, and abuse in care workers' daily lives and workplaces, including the lives of domestic workers who are not a part of an advocacy organization, with whom I also conducted participant observation and interviews. I argue that without DWU's ongoing solidarity, the labor laws that DWU members fought for would be ineffective and almost meaningless, due in large part to broader changes in the political and economic landscape of the United States and across the world during the time that DWU members fought for passage of the Domestic Workers' Bill of Rights. In doing so, this ethnography describes how domestic workers like Katherine from the Preface, who performed the employer's instructions as a poem, and all those in the audience during that DWU meeting can overcome structural employment factors and interpersonal hostility to advocate for themselves and their fellow workers to improve their working conditions in the context of neoliberalism.

It's All Care

A post on my Twitter timeline proclaimed, "It's all care," referencing the presumed distinctions between house-cleaning, childcare, and eldercare positions. Indeed, the boundaries are permeable between cleaning the kitchen, doing laundry, cooking dinner, packing lunches, bathing children or elderly adults, taking out trash, feeding babies, changing diapers, vacuuming, supervising children, and providing companionship and assistance to elderly adults. This book contains stories of weekly housecleaners who eventually move in with their elderly clients to provide around-the-clock care, and of nannies who wash pots and pans each Monday morning after the children in their care board the school bus, examples that show how domestic workers' roles shift and expand to meet the needs of the families for whom they care.

I use the terms *care work* and *domestic work* interchangeably throughout this book primarily because the women I worked with and interviewed used these labels interchangeably as well, as they moved between different job roles over the course of their careers. And, like many of the decisions I have made about framing my research in this book, I follow DWU's lead in also using these terms interchangeably to underline workers' sense of shared circumstances across roles. *Domestic work* generally refers to household labor—cleaning, cooking, caring for children, and assisting and caring for elderly adults in their private residences. The work required to maintain a home and care for its inhabitants often is unpaid labor done by family members, most often women. But typically, the phrase *domestic work* signals paid professionals who clean and care in a non-family member's home. *Care work* can also encompass these same tasks and responsibilities, and includes the care provided by nurses, certified nursing assistants, home health aides, companions to the elderly, and personal attendants in long-term living facilities, nursing homes, and medical institutions like hospitals.

Scholars also consider care as something less literal, almost poetic. In this sense, *care* can connote an internal orientation toward others or the application of focused attention (as in "to take great care with a task") (Stacey 2011). Or, as Christina Sharpe (2018, 180) argues, it can mean "shared risk" or solidarity. The activists in DWU and their allies across the United States care deeply in this sense as well. As we will see through their efforts to recruit, educate, mobilize, feed, and entertain one another and their allies across other employment industries while fighting to improve care work conditions, DWU members' solidarity activism is a form of care for themselves and for one another. Their political platform and activism are, in fact, premised on the notion that care should be as much a core societal value as it is a growing U.S. employment niche. In their day-to-day actions as well as in their historic legislative victory in passing the United States' first-ever labor law for domestic workers, DWU members enact the idea of care as shared risk, fighting alongside and for their fellow workers and allies, even—as we will see—when they are overworked, tired, and disillusioned themselves.

Care work is a growing field in the United States and around the world. There are approximately two million workers employed in private homes as childcare or eldercare providers and housecleaners in the United States, providing care "from cradle to grave," as domestic work advocates often say (Wolfe et al. 2020). One of DWU's board members and a full-time nanny explained the demand for domestic and care work to me as "huge" and growing:

The need for domestic workers in this country—it's huge. Not only are we providing care for babies and young children and young adults, but also as they continue to age or as their parents continue to age then we're providing the eldercare for them in another aspect of life. Between the youth and the aging gracefully part, many times a lot of these employers need someone to maintain their homes as well. That's where we come in between the nannies, the housekeepers, or the elderly care providers.

Most of these workers—a little more than half—care for elderly people in their homes, providing assistance with walking, eating, toileting, dressing, and bathing (Wolfe et al. 2020). Often eldercare workers shop and prepare meals, clean, help maintain a daily rhythm, and offer companionship. Depending on the client's needs and the worker's official title—whether an elder companion, personal attendant, certified nursing assistant (CNA), or home health aide (HHA)—they may also administer medication and take vital signs. Childcare providers likewise fulfill a variety of roles caring for children and babies, providing transportation, supervision, and social engagement for the children in their care, and often assuming some cleaning, cooking, and laundry tasks as well. Housecleaners often work for more than one family, providing weekly or monthly cleaning services and shuttling from one home to another in any given day or week.

Women, and women of color in particular, predominate in these crucial care work roles. More than 90 percent of domestic workers in the United States are women (Wolfe et al. 2020). Moreover, women of color account for just over half of those working as domestic workers nationally (Wolfe et al. 2020). In New York City, 78 percent of household workers were born outside of the United States (National Domestic Workers Alliance, n.d.). Linda Burnham, research director of the National Domestic Workers Alliance, and Nik Theodore (2012, 4), professor of urban planning, write:

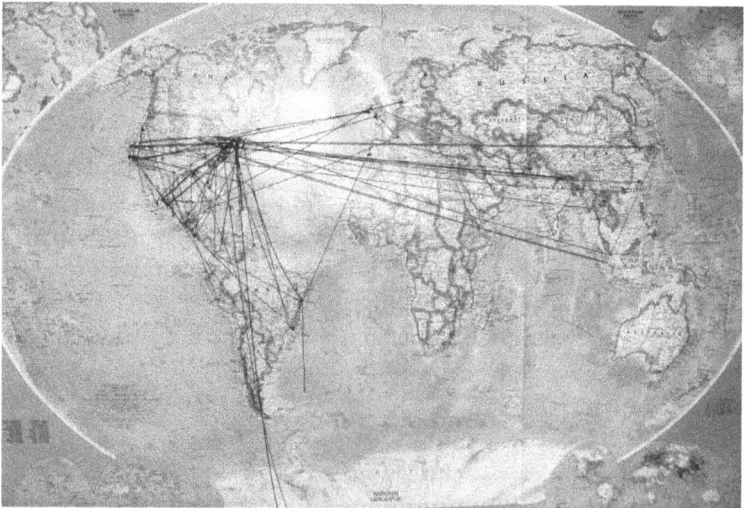

Figure I.2 Image of a map displayed at the convention, illustrating domestic workers' migratory paths using differently colored string.

The reasons women leave their native countries are as varied as the women themselves; each woman's story is filled with unique hopes and heartaches. Yet, their individual decisions animate a global movement of labor: the unstoppable migrations of workers from severely distressed economies to economies that benefit from their hard work.

In other words, though women's reasons for engaging in domestic work may vary, foreign economies benefit from their labor while global economic policies that largely benefit U.S.-based transnational corporations create conditions that necessitate women's migration abroad. At the same time, as Katherine's performance described in the Preface reveals, domestic workers face challenges working in private homes, such as irregular schedules, tension over job roles, and abrupt termination, which have only been exacerbated in the context of the COVID-19 pandemic. As frontline workers, domestic workers have borne the brunt of several overlapping crises, including increased exposure to COVID-19 on the job, rising unemployment, and resulting eviction and food insecurity.

Domestic Workers United

DWU is a membership organization providing legal assistance and nanny training to its members while organizing domestic workers to bring "dignity and respect" to household labor (Nadasen 2009a). The group formed in 1999 under the auspices of two other advocacy groups: the Committee Against Anti-Asian Violence and Andolan, which, according to activists, means "movement" in several South Asian languages. Recognizing that their members worked as nannies and elderly companions, both groups formed worker projects to address the conditions in the industry. They soon joined with Caribbean women and later with Latina domestic workers who were not yet formally organized in labor or cultural organizations.

Together, this loose collection of groups and communities formed the New York Domestic Worker Justice Coalition. In early meetings, workers met in libraries and parks to identify the key issues affecting their sector. Early campaigns targeted individual employers who withheld wages, abused workers, restricted their movement, and con-

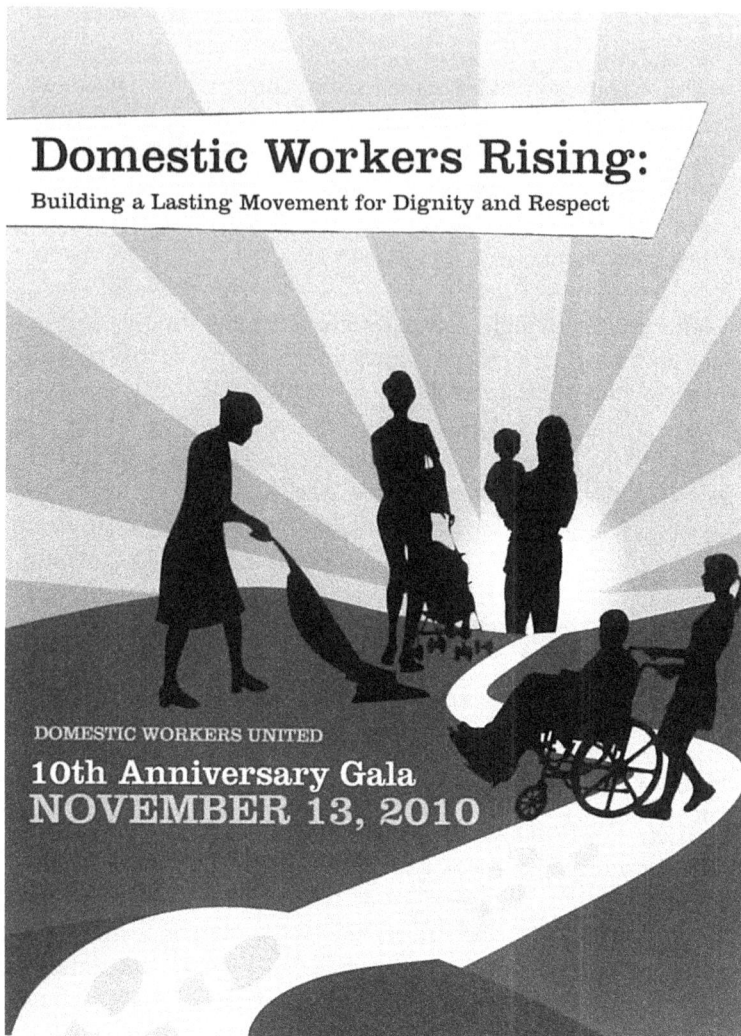

Figure I.3 Cover of the program for the DWU tenth anniversary gala.

fiscated their official documents. The campaign to win a Domestic Workers' Bill of Rights began in 2002, at New York's first domestic worker convention. Allison, a longtime DWU member, was quoted in the gala materials, saying that the convention was the "brain behind the Bill of Rights, where it was born."

DWU members are nannies, caregivers, and housecleaners who participate in the organization as volunteer activists and who pay dues to help keep its operations running. They are mostly Caribbean women from countries like Barbados, Jamaica, and Trinidad and Tobago. Alongside other ethno-national associations—such as Damayan Filipino Workers' Center and Adhikaar, a Nepalese advocacy organization—DWU's membership reflects the demographic character of the industry.

The group's executive board strives for representational parity of Latina and Caribbean members, who compose the bulk of the organization's four thousand members.[1] During my research from 2010 through 2012, most monthly meetings were attended by about fifty members. At smaller meetings and events, like board meetings or trainings to facilitate the implementation of the new Domestic Workers' Bill of Rights, attendance could range from five to thirty members. Most of the members at that time worked primarily in childcare, but many DWU members oscillated among housekeeping, childcare, and eldercare positions over the course of their careers. For more than a decade, with DWU at its helm, the New York Domestic Worker Justice Coalition fought for the passage of the Domestic Workers' Bill of Rights, and the coalition has continued to fight for domestic worker rights since its 2010 implementation.

Solidarity and Precarity

Studying DWU and the passage of the New York Domestic Workers' Bill of Rights offers us the opportunity to consider what makes domestic work—and the activism of domestic workers—unique, and what lessons workers across industries can draw from their legislative success. Primarily, I think of *Solidarity & Care* as an ethnography of solidarity overcoming precarity. Let me briefly introduce those two terms and their significance to the DWU case—and to all of our lives.

Solidarity is both a belief and a practice, an action on behalf of another. It originates with the Roman law of shared debt, where members of a family or community were equally responsible for one another's financial obligations (Bayertz 1999). Social theorist Jodi Dean (1996, 14) describes solidarity as the recognition and affirmation that, for each of us, our "integrity depends on our relationships with others." It is also the reaction to a particular context: "Solidarity is both a response to, and a direct product of, injustice," writes Magdalena

Sztandara (2021, 241), meaning that solidarity is necessary in response to harmful circumstances facing us or others with whom we choose to align ourselves.[2] For example, when DWU members join together to protest in response to another domestic worker's experience of physical assault, racist attacks, and withholding of wages, they enact the notion that their own integrity is bound up with—even dependent on, as Dean argues—their relationships to others. DWU's protests, performances, and storytelling reinforce the "sense of shared risk" that Sharpe (2018, 180) argues is a critical component of care.

Passing the New York Domestic Workers' Bill of Rights, as we will see, required sustained effort over a decade. Through myriad phases and political campaigns, domestic workers' solidarity kept them going, as they stood together against mistreatment and supported one another in their struggles to achieve "dignity and respect" in the workplace. After the bill's passage, domestic workers realized that both implementing the law and ensuring that individual workers benefited from its provisions would require ongoing efforts to hold employers and politicians accountable, to educate others about what the new law meant, and to continue to care for one another.

Evidencing the reach and importance of DWU's activism, Barbara Ehrenreich, renowned journalist and author of *Nickel and Dimed*, spoke in support of DWU at an April 2009 press conference. She first noted the economic context surrounding the broad multiracial women's labor coalition, recognizing that the situation for most U.S. workers—not ideal in the first place—had deteriorated: "In a time of economic crisis, when people are losing their jobs, when all these bad things are happening to so many American workers, why should this one set of workers have a Bill of Rights guaranteeing things . . . that other workers are losing or perhaps never had?" (quoted in Poo 2011, 50). Ehrenreich then answered her own question: "This would not be the first time that women, and particularly women of color, have taken the lead in labor struggles in this country and showed the rest of us the way to go" (50). With this statement, Ehrenreich alluded to the decades of transformative organizing that women workers have undertaken over the past century, leading the way for improved working conditions across industries.

In the more than ten years that passed since that speech, the economic recession abated but the situation for many U.S. workers continued to worsen or did not improve much. Since the early 1970s, the typical worker's inflation-adjusted hourly wages have risen only 0.2 percent per year (Shambaugh and Nunn 2017). Income inequality— the difference between how much money the very wealthiest Americans earn and the salaries of middle-class or working-class workers—has reached levels seen only during the Gilded Era (Shambaugh and Nunn 2017). Furthermore, since the 1970s, workers across industries, regardless of their job roles, have experienced mounting uncertainty and instability wrought by big, structural changes that we can think of as *neoliberalism* and by employers' efforts to reduce wages and eliminate benefits through overseas outsourcing where possible, and through casualization, deskilling, and fragmentation here in the United States. In Chapter 2, I define *neoliberalism* and trace its ascent over the past four decades. For now, I simply want to introduce a central feature of many contemporary workers' experiences: precarity.

Precarity is a fairly new term, reflecting how closely tied it is to the socioeconomic conditions of the past four decades. French theorist Pierre Bourdieu (1998, 82) first described precarity, writing, "Job insecurity is now everywhere," as illustrated by the increasing "number of temporary, part-time or casual positions . . . making the whole future uncertain." Then, during a 2000 French protest campaign to improve wages and working conditions at McDonald's, activists rallied against what they called the "precarious status" of fast-food employment (Mabrouki and Lebègue 2004). In both of these instances, the term was used in the French language (*précarité*), translating to *insecure employment* or *casualization* in English.

These days *precarity* is commonly used in English as well, recalling the history of its French usage while expanding to encompass other features of contemporary life. Anthropologist Kathleen Millar (2014, 34) defines *precarity* "as states of anxiety, desperation, unbelonging, and risk experienced by temporary and irregularly employed workers." While *precarity* thus encompasses the emotional states of workers whose livelihoods are unstable or insecure, it is also a sociological concept referring to the broader economic conditions that lead to jobs being unstable. In a report on precarity, the International Labour Organization (2015, n.p.) found that globally "three quarters of workers are employed on temporary or short-term contracts, in informal jobs often without any contract, under own-account arrangements or in unpaid family jobs." Anthropologists Jennifer Shaw and Darren Byler (2016) have argued that "precarity as we know it today is a condition of millennial capitalism. This form of capitalism, often described as *neoliberal*, promotes a political logic of radical individuality, self-responsibility, and independence."

Platform- or gig-economy jobs are a prime example of precarity. Typified by Uber and TaskRabbit, *gig economy* refers to the technology-abetted practice of companies, or employers, insulating themselves against economic responsibility for their employees by classifying workers as independent contractors or temporary workers. As anthropologist Ana Croegaert (2020, 40) explains, precarity encompasses "new 'gig economies' and people's efforts to patch together numerous employment strategies in the face of increasingly unstable labor markets" (see also Collins 2014). Gig-economy jobs do not provide workers with benefits historically associated with employment, such as health or unemployment insurance, routine hours, predictable wages, or paid vacation or sick time. And, due to the platform's control over workflow, these jobs do not afford workers much of the control or autonomy that a self-employed business owner might experience.

While precarity now reaches into all U.S. employment sectors, it has long simply been a part of the job for many U.S. care workers. Care workers in private homes and nursing facilities have historically endured these same precarious conditions—minimal legal protections, no job security, erratic schedules, lack of healthcare or retirement insurance, and inadequate or absent sick and vacation time— along with dismally low wages (Nadasen 2015a). Domestic Workers United was formed to resist the long history of precarity in care-sector jobs. Their model has achieved legislative success precisely among the workers long considered the most powerless—migrant women, many undocumented—in an economic climate where stable, dignified work is the exception rather than the rule.

In the face of this widespread precarity, DWU's activism demonstrates what workers can accomplish together. The New York State legislative win spurred the United Nation's passage of the 2011 Domestic Work Convention. Hawaii and California then followed with similar legislation. The Obama Administration included home healthcare providers in the Fair Labor Standards Act, nationally extending minimum wage and overtime pay to this group beginning in January 2015. In December 2018, Representative Pramila Jayapal and then Senator Kamala Harris cosponsored national legislation based on the New York State Domestic Workers' Bill of Rights, and language used in their bill directly references Domestic Workers United and the gains achieved in New York. The much-touted 2021 Build Back Better infrastructure package promised to federally protect and fund eldercare and childcare workers.

The legislative landscape, however, continually changes. The Build Back Better infrastructure package did not become law. In 2015, the New York State Labor Department reversed the Obama Administration's overtime guarantees for home healthcare workers. Conflicting rulings from federal courts have upheld the indemnity of third-party subcontractors, meaning that employment agencies, for example, can exclude home health aides from overtime and wage theft protections. Despite DWU's and others' successes, wages for care workers have fallen over the past decade to just under $12 per hour (Campbell 2017). My choice to focus on DWU's case is not about its legislative victories—the enforcement of which will always depend on political will and the staffing of federal and state offices—but about domestic workers and those who support them coming together in solidarity activism. I like to think of my writing this book as an act of solidarity with DWU activists and with workers in all sectors.

Ethnography with Care Workers

DWU's precedent-setting legislative success in passing the Domestic Workers' Bill of Rights garnered academic and popular attention long before the 2010 gala, where I met many of its stalwart supporters. There had been a palpable groundswell of enthusiasm for the passage of the Domestic Workers' Bill of Rights. When I began my research that summer of 2010, there were at least two other PhD students researching the organization for their theses and three college student interns studying the organization for their term papers. Given all of the interest in DWU, the group had established a quid pro quo protocol for the growing number of labor-minded researchers interested in their work. I had planned to ask if I could volunteer for the organization as a way to meet domestic worker activists, but their outreach coordinator beat me to it, explaining that I would also become an intern for the organization. Sociologist Tamara Mose Brown (2011, 131) was met with the same request during her ethnographic research on Caribbean childcare providers' use of Brooklyn public spaces to create community; when she contacted Domestic Workers United, the member with whom she spoke also asked her to volunteer with the organization "in return for information." Volunteering provided unexpected benefits, Brown found: phone banking gave her an enlightened sense of the time and labor DWU members dedicated to the group's mission (131).

My role as an intern provided me with much-needed structure, especially early in my ethnographic research while I was still searching for stable housing and couch surfing with family, friends, and friends of friends. My anthropological interest in studying women workers in New York City originated in my own commitment to activism. Years before I ever began conducting research, I learned about Domestic Workers United from their longtime collaborators at Jews for Racial and Economic Justice, where I worked in 2005. Since that time, I had turned my political activism—inside labor unions and social justice organizations in North Carolina, New York, and Michigan—into research questions. Where were working women fighting against economic exploitation, racism, and gendered injustice? How were those struggles going? Obviously, I thought, DWU members and staff could offer some answers to those questions.

For more than two years, I volunteered approximately two days per week in the DWU office, performing a wide range of tasks, from phone banking to website management. I also helped with major events (like their tenth anniversary gala, where I assisted with setup and catering) and ran around large hotels with other volunteers and staff arranging logistics for national conferences. I attended and documented weekly, monthly, and annual meetings of members, executive boards, Department of Labor representatives, politicians, parents, and workers. I recorded trainings, informal gatherings, and events hosted privately by members.

I think of these intern activities as participant observation, cultural anthropology's hallmark method. Participant observation typically entails participating in and observing cultural and social groups, phenomena, or events, typically through longer-term engagement in a community. Often anthropologists immerse themselves in the lives of the people they are studying by living and working in the same way that those people do, day in and day out, for a year or more. Initially I was worried that I was *doing* more than *observing*. Because I spent so much time engaged in volunteer and activist tasks, my research notes include intricate details on, for example, how we planned, prepared, and ran a special meeting, and how I managed the flow of traffic to and from the meeting space, rather than the details of the discussions that took place. Anthropologist Aimee Cox (2015) cleverly inverted the phrase *participant observation*—describing herself as an *observing participant*—to highlight her own active, professional role inside a young women's homeless shelter in Detroit, Michigan. Cox worked in a number of capacities for the organization, eventually becoming its director.

Cox's concept of *observing participant* usefully frames my own research activities as well. For me, *observing participant* denotes the centrality of my volunteer work as an intern and the day-to-day observations that it facilitated inside DWU. Volunteering as an intern allowed me to familiarize myself with the organization and its members gradually over time. Additionally, DWU members (correctly) read my interest in the organization as evidence of my political alignment with their cause. After several months of volunteering and notetaking at formal DWU events, I began to request interviews from individual domestic work activists.

While interning for DWU and documenting their events and meetings, I also met with and conducted interviews with women working across New York City's five boroughs as home health aides, nannies, and elder companions. These workers were not members of DWU and, for the most part, did not envision themselves as part of a workers' movement. To meet these care workers, I took a page from DWU's outreach strategy by approaching them in parks and playgrounds, and on subways and buses to invite them to participate in oral history interviews. I also relied heavily on social-network sampling, asking the workers I interviewed if their friends and colleagues might want to speak with me. Often DWU members would suggest I contact their friends outside of DWU for interviews. Early on, I developed a close relationship with a former home health aide from Mali named Fatou, who returned to home health work shortly after we met, as well as several younger Senegalese and Ivorian women through whom I met the majority of the unaffiliated home health aides and eldercare providers I interviewed.

A Holistic Approach

Once I developed closer friendships with care workers, whether DWU members or unaffiliated, I observed them at their jobs caring for children or adults, attended protests and events with them, and even traveled with them to visit their family members outside of New York City. During my research, I also was employed as an eldercare provider myself (which I have described elsewhere [Glaser 2019]) and, while I did not interview my then coworkers due to concerns about privacy in the workplace, this work provided me with perspectives that shaped the questions I asked and the topics I broached during interviews.

Often anthropologists describe our methods and analyses as *holistic*, meaning that we strive to see the big picture and to understand the broader contexts shaping social realities. Drawing on decades of ethnographic and interdisciplinary research in the United States and the Caribbean, anthropologist Faye Harrison (1991, 36), re-envisioning ethnography, argued that "reworking anthropology highlights the importance of holism, reintegration, and synthesis, which might be characterized as a kind of weaving." Through Harrison's metaphor of weaving, I came to think of the various aspects of my ethnographic research as holistic and connected, despite my participant observation spanning many years, encompassing many different groups of people, and entailing diverse embodied activities, including volunteering and protesting with DWU members and their allies, working as an elder companion, and babysitting for some of the Senegalese families with whom I became quite close.

In this book, I draw on different facets of my ethnographic research for different purposes. First, the majority of this ethnography takes place at DWU's events, inside its meeting rooms, and alongside its members during protest actions. I draw on my firsthand accounts of DWU meetings, trainings, and protests as well as DWU's publications, press releases, and educational materials to trace the path of activist awakening that DWU successfully employs. This aspect of my research also showcases how care workers come together to create change legislatively and how they discuss, debate, and support one another regarding the daily details of their working lives. Second, using interviews and oral histories with DWU members and their allies active in other social justice organizations, I provide history and context for the types of activism that I observed, and I share workers' own words and ideas about how to improve the domestic work sector and about care work's unique barriers to labor organizing. Finally, I include material from interviews with care workers not affiliated with DWU or other labor organizations to give readers a sense of the range of working conditions, interpretations, and impressions that domestic workers shared with me. This comparative approach allows me to consider the same event or issue from the perspective of DWU activists and that of care workers who don't share the organization's political analyses, as I do in Chapter 5.

Social Location inside DWU

Ethnographers have noted that anthropological analyses often rely on a vision of fieldwork in which the ethnographer is expected to "be all-knowing," as anthropologist Ashanté Reese (2019) puts it. Reese (2019) reminds us that "communities can and do control what we see, hear, and do when we are with them in the field." Working inside an established organization made these boundaries somewhat clearer. I understood my responsibilities as an intern and had a sense of which spaces I could access. Because my role as an intern was fairly hands-on, my purview on important moments is deeply situated in a number of ways. Far from being an all-seeing or omnipotent observer, my ethnographic notes reflect particularly placed memories, shaped by where I was physically located in space and what activity I was doing at the time. As a result, most of the chapters in this book open as this one does: by explaining exactly where I was and what I was doing when something noteworthy occurred.

Making explicit my physical location—for example, my position behind a catering table arranging a cheese plate for the gala—also works as a useful metaphor for my location in a sociological sense. *Social location* refers to one's place or position in history and society. It draws attention to how our place in a specific society shapes our worldviews and opportunities, and how it influences how others in that society treat us (Zavella 1991). Like Kimberlé Crenshaw's (1992) concept of *intersectionality*, the notion of *social location* provides a way to conceptualize the compounded influence of racism, sexism, economic exploitation, religious persecution, anti-LGBTQA discrimination, and xenophobia or anti-immigrant oppression on one's life.

The activists in DWU demonstrate an intuitive sense of their social location, uniting women from various parts of the world working in the same employment field. In their framing of DWU as an organization comprising and advocating for "Caribbean, Latina, and African nannies, housekeepers, and elder companions," DWU members situate themselves in the history of the United States' global dominance and ongoing racism. DWU members and their allies also frequently refer to the group members as "immigrant women of color," a phrase that claims a collective social location for their members and other care workers in New York City and across the United States.

My own social location—as a White woman and graduate-student researcher born in the United States to nonimmigrant parents—certainly shaped how I pursued research and influenced how DWU activists, as well as other domestic workers, responded to me. Early on, my language tutor,[3] Aminata, explained to me candidly that "anyone can print a business card and pretend to be a graduate student. How does anyone know you aren't [from] Immigration?" Aminata's instructive comment stayed with me. How could I expect others to trust that I was who I claimed to be? How could I ask others to risk speaking with me, especially given the broader context of New York's punitive immigration policy and its aggressive policing and surveillance of communities of color? Many people appeared to think the risk was too great and declined to speak with me. Others spoke with me only after years of familiarity at DWU events. And others spoke with me precisely because they wanted to amplify the struggle of New York City care workers. They risked speaking with me as an act of political resistance or, as Sharpe (2018) might argue, as an act of care for themselves and other domestic workers. Most of the women I describe in this ethnography spoke with me after we had developed close friendships or professional relationships. In the coming chapters, I include relevant details of my first introductions to the domestic workers with whom I developed closer relationships.

Intimate Habitation and Activist Ethnography

Ethnography entails both participant observation, the data-gathering component of research, and the write-up and analysis of research. Often ethnographers strive to produce a "thick description" of their ethnographic experiences and the people they encountered. This concept was introduced by Clifford Geertz (1973, 6), who writes:

> From one point of view, that of the textbook, doing ethnography is establishing rapport, selecting informants, transcribing texts, taking genealogies, mapping fields, keeping a diary, and so on. But it is not these things . . . that define the enterprise. What defines it is the kind of intellectual effort it is: an elaborate venture in . . . "thick description."

Thick description captures how anthropologists convey both the daily details of their research and the broader context that readers need to reasonably interpret what they've read.

Thick description is the standard for presenting ethnographic research, and I strive to include that level of detail and context in this book. In my classes, my students and I often lament the objectifying tone of anthropological writing, especially in texts where the subject touches close to home (see also Harrison 1991). Performance studies scholar D. Soyini Madison (2010) describes an approach to ethnographic representation called *intimate habitation*, building on the concept introduced by feminist theorist Gayatri Spivak. For Madison, *intimate habitation* means including "the opinions and analyses" of the people with whom we conduct research, by foregrounding their exact words and perceptions "widely and variously woven throughout . . . by direct quotes, verbatim interviews, and oral histories as 'speaking subjects'" (24). Throughout this book, I refer directly to the insights and arguments that DWU members and staff shared with me and with one another at meetings, trainings, and protest actions, as well as in their publications and outreach materials. The theory and history that DWU members drew upon when discussing their own labor in the caring sector often matched closely with what scholars have written about this sector, so I include those references too. Particularly in Chapter 2, I share what I learned at DWU trainings and protests and in conversations with DWU's staff and leadership, to offer a glimpse of the political education that grounds their solidarity activism.

Throughout this book, I try to emulate Madison's methodological and representational approach to intimate habitation by sharing, as much as I can, the words, sentiments, and evolving political opinions of the women and families I studied in order to showcase their process of political solidarity and efforts to improve their labor conditions. And, following Madison, I am frank about my allegiances to the politics, the women, and the friendships I made during my research. These aspects of intimate habitation are also in the tradition of engaged anthropology, which anthropologist Sherry Ortner (2019) describes as "caring deeply about the subject and the people, rather than adopting a stance of detachment." It also seeks to "reveal truths that those in power keep hidden, to promote understanding across cultural and political divides, to provide us with models of grappling with injustice," she notes (Ortner 2019, n.p.).

In my research experience, engaged anthropology also overlaps with activist anthropology, which entails working with and for groups like DWU. Anthropologist Ida Susser (2010, 232) explains the intellectual value of activist ethnography, writing that "participation in efforts for social transformation, working in concert with local grassroots movements, can be documented and analyzed just as with other forms of participant observation, and it is crucial to the development of anthropological theory and practice." As activist anthropologists, Susser suggests, we can analyze and interpret the activism that we support and participate in, assessing what works and what fails, as we advocate for a better world. Sociologist Jennifer Fish (2017 15), who has researched the global movement for domestic workers' legal protections, writes that for scholar-activists, "our work is not our own. . . . It reflects the voices and analyses of people engaged in building a global movement." As a write-up of my research experiences, this book is thus also an act of translation, both in the classic anthropological sense of translating my own observations for readers and in this activist sense that Fish describes. This second sense captures the act of translating and sharing the political arguments and understandings of DWU members and staff, as well as other scholars from history, political science, and sociology, in as direct and clear a manner as I can. As a result, this ethnography is suffused with these engaged, activist approaches, which have shaped the decisions I made in writing it.

In particular, I made two decisions during my ethnographic research that influence how I discuss and represent the women with whom I conducted research. First, except for DWU staff quoted in printed materials (like Gonzalez's gala welcome letter, quoted at the beginning of this chapter), I use aliases for everyone I quote and describe in this book. I made this choice because my notes include both DWU members and care workers who are not involved with any activist organizations. Many of the women I interviewed and observed experienced significant vulnerability[4] in New York, including housing and job insecurity, excessive employer surveillance and oversight, racist harassment, and threats of detention or deportation by U.S. Immigration and Customs Enforcement. To ensure the privacy of the most vulnerable women in my study, I anonymized everyone's identity.

Second, I did not collect data or ask interview questions about immigration status or documentation, though, in some cases, women disclosed their immigration status to me without prompting. Often, participants compared their experiences before and after securing *papers*, meaning the legal authorization to work and live in the United States. Sometimes they privately lamented the risks of working without legal documentation. Other times, we worked together to advance their efforts to secure papers and prepare for citizenship exams. And, in still other situations, they casually mentioned their loved ones who had been detained. When relevant, I include details that were shared with me. But there were many instances when the women with whom I spoke did not broach their immigration status and I did not inquire about it.

This choice was inspired by DWU's activism and analysis, through which the organization draws workers together across migration status, race, and job role. DWU activists fearlessly assert their rights and fight to protect the rights of others, regardless of citizenship status. In part, this is because U.S. labor law covers all workers, regardless of their legal citizenship status (ACLU, n.d.; Brown 2011, 136). But it is also a strategy to build solidarity. The vagaries of domestic work and the laws that shape it apply to all women working in this field, regardless of citizenship status, country of origin, or possession of a work visa, a fact emphasized by DWU activists in trainings and printed materials. One's legal citizenship status should not determine whether one receives labor law protections, fair wages, or dignity in the workplace, or whether one is safe from abuse and harassment. By not inquiring about immigration status, I hope to reinforce the principle that all workers deserve dignity and respect. As a labor activist proclaimed many years prior to the Domestic Workers' Bill of Right's passage at a labor union convention I attended, "There are no illegal people—we are all workers!"

Theoretically, I think of my decision to not inquire about immigration status as an application of anthropologist Audra Simpson's (2017) concept of *ethnographic refusal*. Simpson developed this concept during her ethnographic research on nationhood and citizenship among the Native North American Mohawk Nation, who as she writes refused the imposition of Canadian laws in creative ways, causing debates over identity and group membership. Simpson (2017, 73) notes that, "in such a context, I knew that there were limits to what I could ask—and then what I could say—within the scope of my project on Mohawk nationhood. . . . And so it was that I wrote an ethnography that pivoted upon refusal(s)." For Simpson, "these refusals speak volumes, because they tell us when to stop" (78). The process of writing ethnography entails making decisions about sharing what we asked, or did not ask, as interviewers. And, in this way, refusal is generative (78; see also McGranahan 2016, 320). I hope that my refusal to gather data on domestic workers' immigration statuses, like DWU's activism, generates new ways of considering—and overcoming—categories that allow for the exploitation of workers and curtail solidarity and freedom. In the following chapters, we will follow DWU members and their allies as they refuse the limits set by decades of exclusionary labor policies, economic exploitation, racism, and gendered oppression in the domestic sector. We will also accompany them as they navigate the new terrains created by their activism.[5]

Roadmap: From Isolation to Solidarity

I have organized this book to reflect how I understand the trajectory of domestic workers, as they move from isolation and precarity to activism and solidarity. It is an attempt to replicate my own introduction to care work and DWU's activism, and to retrace, as meaningfully as I can, the steps and strategies that built DWU's solidarity leading up to and since the passage of the New York Domestic Workers' Bill of Rights in 2010. In Chapter 1, I outline some of the specific issues that care workers encounter on the job to provide a sense of the isolation and idiosyncrasies of domestic work jobs, as well as the strategies that allowed DWU members to find one another and overcome the isolation of in-home labor positions. Chapter 2 takes us inside DWU trainings to understand their political education and to historicize the domestic work industry in the United States. My hope is that I can provide readers a glimpse of what they might glean by attending one of these trainings themselves. In Chapter 3, we follow domestic work activists as they apply their political education to the formation of a new law, the Domestic Workers' Bill of Rights. Through DWU members' oral histories, Chapter 3 provides a sense of what fighting for the passage of the Domestic Workers' Bill of Rights entailed and how DWU members came together to ensure that the law could be meaningfully applied inside private homes. Chapter 4 describes how DWU used narrative and emotional appeals to build the coalition of religious communities, employers of domestic workers, labor union members, and politicians first to pass and then to enforce the new law. In Chapter 5, I describe DWU meetings, protests, and events to showcase how solidarity and unity operate in this organization, offering an account of how DWU's activism resonates beyond their group's membership by describing solidarity rallies supporting two abused domestic workers in New York in two drastically different cases. Finally, the Conclusion summarizes lessons that we may take from DWU's approach to solidarity activism in precarious times, and the Epilogue addresses the ongoing effects of the COVID-19 pandemic on care workers and other essential workers.

1

Precarious Caring and Collective Complaints

Overcoming the Isolation and Personalism
of Domestic Work

n 2007, a wealthy Long Island, NY, couple were found guilty on
charges of involuntary servitude, conspiracy, forced labor, and har-
boring undocumented immigrants under a 2000 law that bans human trafficking in the United States.* Two domestic workers, immigrant women from Indonesia, had accused the couple of enslaving
them for five years following the expiration of their temporary work
visas, withholding food, forcing them to work around the clock and
sleep on mats on the floor, and confining them to the home in which
they were forced to labor (Kilgannon 2007; Vitello 2007). Discussing the case with Pamela, a thirty-five-year-old Jamaican eldercare
provider and new DWU member, she told me, "That's always been
my fear, living in somebody's house locked up." Pamela and I met
while folding program books for DWU's tenth anniversary gala. We
developed an especially close friendship working on DWU projects
together, and we spent time together outside of DWU as well, visiting
art museums and socializing in the trendy parts of Brooklyn. Over
the years that I have known Pamela, she has rotated between live-in
eldercare work, temporary waitstaff positions, and long periods of
unemployment. As we will see in this chapter, her insights on eldercare positions have deeply influenced my own perceptions of these
job roles.

I begin this chapter by describing some of the injustices associated with domestic work, relying on care workers' experiences as related during meetings, conversations with me, and formal interviews. First, I draw on my discussions with DWU members as well as scholarly accounts of care work to highlight the exploitative and, in some cases, abusive effects of isolation, especially when domestic workers are undocumented and living in the homes where they work. Second, I discuss personalism in the care work industry, meaning the central role of personal relationships rather than formal agreements, drawing on well-established studies of this feature of care work. I describe how DWU members identify both personalism and power dynamics in private homes as a source of exploitation. The prevalence of personalism in caretaking jobs, which I explain in the next section, encourages care workers to make judgments, or complaints, about their employers, rather than file formal workplace grievances to confront the inequities of their work arrangements. I pay special attention to a Department of Labor hearing I attended with May, a nanny and DWU member, in the wake of the Domestic Workers' Bill of Rights' implementation, as an example of how domestic workers deploy complaints against individual employers. Such complaints, I argue, are shielded appeals for justice, though they are, in isolation, ineffective for redressing workplace issues. I then introduce DWU's recruitment and meetings, like the one at which Katherine performed the employment advertisement as described in the Preface, to argue that DWU's solidarity activism creates a basis for domestic worker activism and community, transforming individual judgments into what I refer to as *collective complaint*. Such collective complaint allows care workers to compare employment circumstances and share strategies for managing their labor, building a strong basis for domestic worker labor solidarity and activism.

Injustices Associated with Domestic Work

Isolation Issues

One of the most persistent challenges in protecting domestic workers and those they care for is the location of domestic work: the isolated and private spaces of someone's home. Scholars argue that working alone in a private home while cleaning, caring for children, or providing healthcare to elderly or infirm adults eliminates or limits domestic workers' connection to coworkers, community, and culture, making these jobs especially taxing and potentially exploitative (Brown 2011; Buch 2015; Coe 2019; Dill 1994; Rollins 1985). As Brown (2011, 37) points out, "isolation is the one factor that uniquely distinguishes domestic childcare from other forms of paid childcare and work in general." Isolation prevents workers from coming together to advocate for themselves or from leveraging the power of their expertise and experience in on-the-job negotiations with employers (37), leaving workers with "few options for constructing an identity outside the work they do" (3). And, as anthropologist Cati Coe (2019, 51) writes, based on her research among African home-based care workers in Washington, DC, such isolation can cause domestic workers to view "their work as prisonlike because of the restrictions on their movement and activities, the result of having to be with the patient at all times." As we will see, domestic care workers' isolation exacerbates other unequal facets of their employment experiences.

This isolation has several implications for workers (as well as for those they care for), the most egregious of which is workers' exposure to harassment and abuse. Abuse and exploitation are unfortunately not uncommon in care work arrangements. Sometimes abuse can come from the people being cared for: Coe (2019, 24) found that nursing home administrators feared that care workers might sue over the abuse they suffered from nursing home residents, citing this as a reason for denying Coe access to the facility. When occurring in a private residence, abuse and harassment, whether coming from the employer or the person being cared for, often remain unseen and unreported. Between 2011 and 2012, the National Domestic Workers Alliance, a national advocacy organization, surveyed and interviewed thousands of domestic workers across fourteen metropolitan regions in the United States and found that 20 percent of all domestic workers interviewed had experienced demeaning, violent, and racist treatment from their employers (Burnham and Theodore 2012, 40).[1] For domestic workers living in the homes where they worked, verbal abuse and assault were even more common, approaching 40 percent (40).[2]

As the 2007 enslavement case illustrates, living in the home of one's employer entails risk of confinement, mistreatment, and neglect of basic necessities like food, heat, water, and a comfortable place to sleep (Adams and Dickey 2000; Glenn 2012). I met Amy, a Guinean live-in certified nursing assistant, in 2012 through a DWU member related to Amy's employer. I traveled to visit Amy at her employer's Bronx apartment during her physical therapy appointments when Amy stayed behind straightening up and preparing meals for later that afternoon. Amy slept at her employer's apartment four nights of the week, traveling between her employer's place in the Bronx and her Long Island home via public transportation each Sunday and Thursday morning. This job was difficult for Amy—her patient was an elderly woman with dementia who yelled and struck her on occasion—and she seemed to welcome my company. Amy and I sat at a round bistro-style table in the corner of a small kitchen as we talked. In the tiny apartment, I could see a den with a recliner chair, small sofa, and television. I could also see the narrow hallway that I assumed led to multiple bedrooms. I asked Amy how she slept, and she pointed to the recliner chair in the corner. "There isn't a bedroom?" I asked in disbelief. "See, just this one," she replied taciturnly, walking with me down the short hallway to peer into her patient's bedroom. Careful to not betray her patient's privacy or to enter her private space, Amy quickly gestured for me to return to the common area before explaining that during the nights she worked here, she slept on the recliner while her patient slept in the sole bedroom in a hospital-outfitted bed. "Oh, you sleep on a recliner," I reflected back to her in a somber tone, realizing how unconformable her sleeping arrangements were. "Is that permitted . . . by your company?" I asked. Amy told me that, while it wasn't ideal, the company employing her didn't require families to furnish beds or other suitable sleeping surfaces for live-in care workers.

Even DWU members who had not experienced abuse or confinement in the homes where they worked had heard of or witnessed cases where domestic workers encountered abuse, neglect, confinement, and in some cases death. Mary, a full-time nanny and active DWU member, recounted a story during my initial interview with her that still haunts me. Explaining to me that her working conditions were satisfactory, she added that as an activist she had heard many experiences of hardship. "There are people who will say 'I have a story to tell' . . . I meet people like that," she told me. "I know somebody who died in there," Mary confided, when discussing a live-in housekeeping position that she had left years earlier. "When I left there, I left her there," she said solemnly of the live-in caretaker alongside whom she worked, and continued, "She died in that house, because she had asthma and then living with the cats, inhaling the cat hair and living in the basement with the freezer and all these things." Growing more concerned, she asked me, "You understand? I don't know what the basement was like for her." As an asthmatic myself, I often find myself thinking of Mary's final phrase—"I don't know what the basement was like for her"—in moments just before I reach for my rescue inhaler. I can't help but dwell on how many more stories there must be of unsanitary, unsafe, and sweltering or frigid living and working conditions, hidden away in basements and spare rooms and on pullout sofas and rollaway beds. By Mary's account, this caretaker's death was not the result of malice but rather her employers' neglect and the desperation for employment that drives many women into unsafe live-in working situations.

Precarious Citizenship and Unsafe Live-in Work

Pamela attributed her live-in eldercare positions directly to the precariousness of her citizenship status and financial circumstances. On a winter afternoon outing to Downtown Brooklyn, she told me, "I've been an immigrant most of my life." She had been living in New York City, she emphasized, for "ten years now. Ten years, I'm not talking about the times I visited; I'm ten years living [here]," she said. Despite her decade-long Brooklyn residency, Pamela lived in the United States without documentation, having "overstayed" a temporary travel visa she obtained in her twenties. Like many Caribbean migrants, Pamela immigrated to New York to reunite with her mother who had migrated years earlier when Pamela was a teenager.

Pamela analyzed her migration and employment experiences as representative of broader shifts in migration, geopolitics, and economy. As an activist and DWU member, she was both inclined toward a social justice interpretation of these structural factors and exposed to trainings and political demonstrations that further contextualized and historicized them, which I describe in detail in Chapter 2. During one of our 2011 visits to the Occupy Wall Street encampment in Zuccotti Park, for example, Pamela told me:

And then they use immigration against us, because—when I read this Marx book, [he argues that] alienation of the worker leads to exploitation, so when you have your immigration status over, you are alienated, you feel minimized, you won't stand up for your rights.

In this quote, Pamela refers to an argument made by Karl Marx in *Economic and Philosophic Manuscripts of 1844* ([1932] 1961), in which he contends that because workers have to sell their labor to afford basic necessities, they are alienated—or separated—from their human nature and from the pleasure of laboring to produce something simply because they want to. Pamela wisely expanded this idea of alienation to include a condemnation of the particularly exploitative circumstances that undocumented immigrants experience: "When you have your immigration status over, you are alienated." Immigrants without official immigration documentation can face deportation or detention, and Pamela connected this fact to the fear of punitive immigration policies that may discourage workers from standing up for themselves. And, in fact, across industries, employers do use the threat of deportation to retaliate against immigrant workers who stand up for their rights in the workplace (Smith, Avendaño, and Ortega 2009).

Although Pamela did not use the term *precarity* in her analysis, she perfectly explained its interwoven facets—psychological, legal, and economic vulnerability—as discussed in the Introduction. Her statement reveals Pamela's sensitivity to her own and other women's psychological dispositions resulting from these insecurities ("you feel minimized"), and she repeatedly demonstrated this sense of shared vulnerability throughout our time together. Characteristic of her introspective nature, Pamela also explained that her financial and legal insecurity amplified "anxiety issues [that] stem from having a father dying at five years old."

Recounting her erratic employment past, she explained that she located eldercare employment through an agency in Brooklyn, the same agency that her mother and other women in her circle used for temporary employment. The agency placed women in private homes for a period of three weeks—during which they work around the clock—followed by one week off. The isolation of these live-in place-ments concerned Pamela, who worried she would be trapped, unable to leave her employer's home.

Her decision to pursue a live-in caregiving job represented a point of financial desperation. At the time of our conversation, Pamela was on the brink of losing her apartment and was anxious and frustrated with the dead-end positions that she and her family members accepted to "stay afloat." She complained, "I got a job from them. It didn't even last two months. They're a bunch of thieves, a bunch of thieves. You know, and that's the trap with them. We pay them to get a job, and they treat us like shit and always take the employers' sides over us." This employment agency was notorious among DWU members and Caribbean women, earning a reputation for unethical and extractive employment practices targeting undocumented Caribbean immigrants.[3] Coe (2019, 226) also found that care workers were aware of placement agencies' lucrative business model: agencies typically have low operational overhead, yet charge families double the hourly rate paid to care workers.

Describing how the isolation of domestic work exacerbates the structural vulnerability many care workers experience—e.g., as undocumented migrant workers—Pamela argued that employment agencies benefit from the chronic insecurity and vulnerability facing immigrant women. Their lack of documentation prevents workers from accessing employment opportunities elsewhere, forcing them into undesirable, often dangerous working conditions. Pamela recalled her friend Bev's experience with a live-in eldercare position. Bev was another Caribbean woman with tenuous employment and citizenship status. "I remember I hadn't seen Bev for a while in the agency," Pamela recalled, "Bev is very scared, very apprehensive, you know." In this case, Bev decided to return home rather than endure the isolation, poor treatment, and uninhabitable living conditions she encountered at her eldercare position. Reviewing the situation, Pamela reflected, "Some women come on a visa for six months, do the work, then go back home. They're going back home, they say, 'because I can't take the shitty behavior forever.' You know what I mean?" she asked earnestly. For many domestic workers, like Bev, leaving is the most expedient response to poor treatment and exploitation; again, Coe (2019, 6) similarly identified "exit" as a strategy among the care workers she studied. But, as we will see, it is not often feasible for workers to leave an undesirable work situation even if they would like to.

Around-the-Clock Care

Even in less obviously unsuitable cases, live-in domestic workers often work in unsustainable circumstances. All of the live-in care workers I spoke to, DWU members as well as unaffiliated domestic workers, told me that they did not have any break from their duties. Whether caring for elderly adults or for children and babies, the domestic workers I spoke with consistently mentioned how they spent nights awake caring for their wards. The survey conducted by the National Domestic Workers Alliance found that more than half of live-in care workers worked long hours exceeding an eight-hour workday, which is the standard in the United States (Burnham and Theodore 2012, 30). Twenty-five percent of live-in domestic workers reported getting fewer than five hours of sleep per night, attending to the children and elderly in their care around the clock (30). Yet, 67 percent of live-in workers earned less than minimum wage, with a median hourly wage of only $6.15 (19).

Responding to the evolving needs of those in their care, care workers often found themselves effectively moving into the homes of the families for whom they work, as the needs of the elderly patients or babies in their care expanded beyond a standard eight-hour workday. Pearl, for example, was a Jamaican woman in her early fifties, who joined DWU after the passage of the Domestic Workers' Bill of Rights, learning about the group from extensive news coverage of the bill's provisions. Pearl told me she provided around-the-clock care for "Papa Joe" for about five years in his New Jersey home. "I do everything," she told me. "I clean. I do adult care." When Pearl accepted the role as Papa Joe's care worker, it was not a live-in position, but, as Papa Joe's health deteriorated, Pearl's role grew and grew, until finally she was sleeping at his home most nights. At first, she caught a few hours' sleep on a recliner chair when Papa Joe dozed off. But, eventually, she sat beside him throughout the night. "He lived to be ninety-five, and Joe had all his faculties," she remembered. "His body was decaying. But his mind was sharp. But you got no sleep. The last three or four months before he passed, oh, my God. He'd call for you the whole night, 'Pearl, Pearl.' Then, his voice got so weak. I bought him a bell so he could ring. And he would just want a cup of tea, 'Just talk to me. Just sit up with me.' And my eyes are falling down."

Papa Joe's family paid Pearl a set weekly salary and did not require her to record how many hours she worked. Her work week far exceeded forty hours per week as she sat with Joe through his sleepless nights. Pearl's long nights accompanying Papa Joe, "as he got sicker and sicker and sicker and sicker," as she recalled, were effectively unremunerated. His adult daughter extracted Pearl's around-the-clock care and companionship by appealing to Pearl's fondness for Joe as well as her sympathy for his circumstances. "You're all he knows," Pearl reported the daughter beseeching, "You can't leave him." Pearl was visibly weary as she recounted the nights she sat with Joe and the complicated emotional obligation she felt both to him and to his daughter. "But my care was with him," she remembered, "until he passed."

As Pearl's poignant account illustrates, the live-in care worker arrangement frequently degrades workers' pay and compensation by extracting care around the clock. Pearl's attachment to Joe and her compassion in providing him with constant companionship in his final months exemplify another feature of care work: *personalism*, a term scholars use to describe the personal relationships that naturally develop between caretakers and the children or adults for whom they care, or between caretakers and their employers (Buch 2013; Hondagneu-Sotelo 2001). Personalism often disadvantages workers, who feel a sense of obligation and concern for their wards, encouraging them to work additional hours or days without pay, just as Pearl did.

Personalism

Scholars use the concept of *personalism* to describe the character of employer-employee relations in the U.S. care-work sector. It is related to the notion of *relational labor* meaning *emotional attunement* on the part of the caregiver, as well as to the reciprocal emotional connections between caregivers and those for whom they work (Buch 2013; Duffy 2011; Twigg 2000). The relational aspects of care work are critically important. And, based on conversations I had with domestic workers and with employers, they are meaningful to all parties as well. DWU members, for example, often explained that they did not want to sacrifice the relational aspects of their jobs to standardize their working conditions. As we will see in Chapter 4, amplifying the relational labor of domestic workers was a key strategy that domestic worker activists used to motivate others to join with them and enforce the new laws covering domestic work. Similarly, at a meeting of domestic workers, parents, and activists that I attended, the group uniformly agreed that while care work undoubtedly requires professional skill and some formal agreements, like employment contracts and standard working hours, it is unlike other forms of work due to the intimacy and closeness that often develop between caregivers and patients, families, and children.

However, scholars argue that these types of emotional attachments, while natural and very common in care work, extract unpaid "emotional labor" (Hochschild 1983) from workers by exploiting their intrinsic empathy (Glenn 1992). In her pioneering research on African American housecleaners' relationships with their female employers, sociologist Judith Rollins (1985, 156) argues that "the precise elements that make [domestic work] unique: the personal relationship between employee and employer" make domestic work more exploitative than comparable jobs. Sociologist Shireen Ally (2009, 99) describes these types of arrangements as "personalized relations of service," observing that employers often use emotional closeness to manipulate workers or to compel them to work longer hours.

The exploitative aspects of personalism are captured in the "one of the family" trope, a way researchers describe employers' use of kinship terminology and a sense of familial obligation to relate to household employees (Romero 1992). As I discuss in Chapter 2, this trope dates back to the period of U.S. slavery and surfaces in nearly all accounts of domestic work that I have read and among both unaffiliated domestic workers and DWU members in New York. Formal training programs, for example, encourage eldercare providers to "think of the patients like your mother" (Diamond 1992, 88), in the hope that, as sociologist Mignon Duffy (2011, 89) argues, "Relational obligations will compel Certified Nursing Assistants to go above and beyond their defined duties." Mary Romero (1992, 43), who wrote one of the foundational studies on U.S. domestic work, points out that "the more personal service is included in the domestic's daily work, the more emotional labor is extracted and the more likely the employer will insist that the domestic is 'one of the family.'"

Jean, a longtime nanny, explained this phenomenon to me this way: "I have realized as a nanny that you can get caught up in a love for their kids, that sometimes you tend to ignore ill treatment from the employers." Describing a previous position, Jean told me, "They had a newborn baby. And his name was, oh my God, Eric. Eric is still in my life. Eric became my child." Jean was visibly pleased as she recollected her fondness for Eric. Her affection for him positively affected her job satisfaction and performance during the years she cared for him, which benefited her employers (Eric's parents) because they knew she would be a reliable caretaker. Her emotional closeness to Eric provided his parents with security and peace of mind, and it assured them of her continued affection and care. Brown (2011, 17) found that, due to the personalism of their roles, "childcare providers slip into family metaphors" when discussing the families for whom they work, just as Jean did when describing Eric as "her child." And as Jean's example illustrates, relying on workers' emotional investments in their charges permits parents to maximize the caretaking arrangement. The emotional bond between caretakers and the children or the elderly adults in their care often discourages the base negotiation of terms, as I describe in the next section.

On Rocking the Boat: Private Homes and Power Imbalances

Domestic workers in New York individually lack the negotiating power to directly influence job duties, wages, and hours in domestic work positions precisely because they work alone, isolated in private homes, in personalized relationships.[4] Domestic worker advocates decry the industry as being unfairly stacked against employees in the "one employer to one employee" arrangement. "This industry is such an isolated industry," Helen, a DWU leader and full-time nanny, explained to me, as we sat in Brooklyn's Fulton Mall at a small round table on the crowded second-floor café of a Barnes and Noble. Analyzing the circumstances facing childcare workers, she pointed out that "oftentimes, the workers are negotiating with two employers. It's always that uneven balance . . . working for a family, absolutely." Helen meant that in her work experience (and in the experiences of other care workers she knew) the employer was typically a married couple, which meant that she had to negotiate and deal with two employers. Unlike in commercial or industrial workplaces, where workers usually outnumber managers, bosses, or owners, domestic workers do not work alongside others with whom they can sympathize and strategize. Instead, domestic workers are very often outnumbered by the parents and family members who employ them to care for their children, elderly relatives, or homes.

Working for a private family guarantees worker isolation and an attendant power imbalance. Termination is a constant possibility, as families are not required to provide notice or severance pay in any U.S. state. When workers attempt to assert concrete employment demands and obtain a clear set of expectations regarding job duties and remuneration, employers often pass them over, explaining that they prefer to hire someone "more flexible" instead, as was the case for Jewel. When we spoke, Jewel was a Jamaican woman in her early fifties, and she had spent the better part of two decades living in New York City. A longtime nanny, she had been unemployed for several months when we met for coffee in September 2011. As a result, she had lost her Bronx apartment and moved to New Jersey to live with a friend. Jewel lamented her prolonged unemployment, explaining that her professionalism and sophistication in job interviews upended employers' expectations: "They want a 'Yes, ma'am,' someone they can boss around." A distinctly Southern form of acquiescence, the phrase "Yes, ma'am" evokes the racialized hierarchy of U.S. domestic service during the period of slavery and beyond, as Rollins has argued. In her research, Rollins (1985, 161) found that linguistic deference provides domestic work employers with a sense of superiority and comfort in their employee-employer relations. Further, Rollins argues that, like Jewel, domestic workers are aware of their employers' race-based expectations of elaborate deference rituals—such as hierarchical address and naming conventions, and curtailed movement—and accommodate them to attain or keep jobs (158). Coe (2019, 114) also writes that employers—and even elderly patients or children in the care of domestic workers—"may seek to exert control through racist and sexist insults, humiliation, or discourses of being the boss."

Control over workplace responsibilities, therefore, represents a way for care workers both to resist oppression and domination in their working relationships and to assert their professional boundaries and expertise. As Jewel observed, her comportment and attitude suggested to employers that she would attempt to exert too much control over her labor, that she would not be "someone they can boss around." Sociologist Cynthia Cranford (2020) argues that care workers often resist relations of domination in home-based employment by limiting their job roles to specific types of tasks—excluding job tasks that they feel demean them or fall outside of their expertise—resulting in what Cranford identified as a time-versus-task tension in domestic work employment. Brown's (2011) research among childcare providers similarly documented case after case of care workers struggling to assert their own preferences in terms of hours, work roles, and dignity on the job.

Jewel connected her assertiveness on a recent job with the circumstances surrounding her eventual termination: "As soon as you see her game and you try to tell her, 'This is not what we do.' Not only was it childcare; she wanted me to clean her dishes and do her grill and the pots and pans that she cooked on Saturday when she entertained. She'd leave them for Monday for me." Jewel concluded, "That's not what I came here for. I came here for the baby," her voice raising in pitch and volume for emphasis. Understanding the addition of extraneous non-child-related tasks as a tactic to exploit her labor, Jewel noted, "If she [her former employer] is paying you money, she'll work you to the bone to make sure she gets every dime out of you." Jewel reported retaliatory dismissal: "Within what? A week and a half or two. After that I was fired—I knew it was coming." Jewel's experience highlights individual domestic workers' valid fears of retaliation, in the form of abrupt termination, for attempting to control their own labor in their workplaces, a key factor that led many domestic workers to DWU.

When I met Danata, a nanny and DWU member from Barbados, she was in her early forties and had been working and living in Brooklyn for nearly a decade, primarily for middle-class, White, U.S.-born families. When we spoke about her work history, she named abrupt termination as her main complaint. I asked her whether she had received any notice of termination. "Not anything," she replied. In one instance, Danata's employer "came back at 3 [P.M.] and fired me. . . . She didn't give me a reason, but I think it's because . . . she didn't like my way of doing things." The employer had left for work as usual but returned early, before 5 P.M., to terminate Danata's employment on her first day. Abrupt termination was an ongoing, stressful issue for Danata. Its significance reflects the economic insecurity of domestic work jobs and the class circumstances of domestic workers, who often live paycheck to paycheck.

As Jewel's and Danata's experiences illustrate, employers' unilateral ability to terminate nannies' employment is an ongoing source of anxiety and uncertainty on the job. While employees across industries may fear termination, domestic workers face greater risk because of the personalism and the isolation of their jobs, which prevent them from negotiating or collectively addressing complaints. Helen elaborated, "This industry is so isolating and it's scary. . . . There's so much at risk even raising the issues." For many women working in private homes, objecting to long working hours or strenuous work tasks is far too risky. Explaining the incentive not to "rock the boat," Helen extrapolated, "Because rocking the boat could mean termination. Termination could mean unemployment. Unemployment means I cannot provide for my family, and there are all of these other chains of events that happen." It is difficult to overstate how stressful potential job loss is for individual domestic workers and how dire the ramifications of unemployment are for them and their families—as evidenced by Jewel's eviction from her apartment and by Pamela's desperation on the brink of losing her apartment, described at the opening of this chapter. And, as Jewel's and Danata's stories each demonstrate, for domestic workers, termination without any explanation is an ever-present threat. Each domestic worker I spoke with, both DWU members and unaffiliated domestic workers, shared a story of being fired in retaliation for their reluctance to take on additional job tasks or being fired without warning for reasons that were never enumerated.

Workers' Judgments

Complaints as Appeals for Justice

The prevalence of personalism in caretaking jobs encourages childcare and eldercare workers to make personal judgments about their employers, rather than file formal workplace grievances, as a way of articulating the inequities of their work arrangements. In the feminized caregiving field, where both employer and employee are likely to be women, personalism reflects the enduring sexual division of household and care labor (Orloff 1993).

Care workers consistently characterized parents, and particularly mothers, as fit or unfit, caring or absent, and devoted or distracted as a means of establishing their employment situation as positive or negative. In my interviews, if a childcare provider described her employer in terms of her poor parenting, she invariably classified the position as undesirable as well. Such judgments emerge from both the personalism and the unequal labor arrangements of caretaking. The tendency for care workers to voice job grievances in terms of their employers' personal or parental failings exposes some of the particular workplace issues that domestic workers encounter in private homes—namely, isolation, personalism, and abrupt termination.

The personalized and individual nature of these employment relationships encouraged nannies, in particular, to informally voice dissatisfaction with their positions, often linking their employers' parenting skills to the desirability of the position. For example, a DWU member described a harrowing babysitting experience in which she had to use infant CPR to resuscitate her young ward, before characterizing the child's mother. She recalled, "All of a sudden, I didn't hear [the baby's] voice anymore. And when I ran to the room, she was blue. She was choking on mucous, and I started doing CPR on the baby, and I couldn't get a pulse. And I just cup her little mouth, her little chin in my hand, as I hit. And I pat her back, like really slap on her back. The mucous she was choking on came out, and I felt so good." This care worker expressed visible relief as she proudly described her use of infant CPR, before continuing on to describe the infant's mother: she began "screaming like I was killing her baby, and she was running down the street like a crazy woman. She was totally neurotic. Sometimes maternal instincts don't click in at the right time." Retelling these stories, whether to me or one another, allows care workers to retrospectively justify and contextualize their own actions—for example, the successful and appropriate use of infant CPR—in spite of employers' flagging appreciation and recognition. This collective retelling of workplace stories provides care workers with a sense of shared work experiences that their isolated worksites otherwise inhibit.

Given the power imbalance between domestic workers and their employers in determining matters like wages, hours, and job duties, we can understand nannies' complaints about their employers' parental shortcomings as shielded appeals for justice. Anthropologists, focusing on medical encounters and legal proceedings, have studied how people use complaints, finding that complaints "invoke certain typified forms of suffering that call for the rectification of perceived injustices" (Buchbinder 2010, 124; see also Ahmed 2017; Chua 2012; Kugelmann 1999). For care workers, complaints about individual employers' inadequacies supplant broader critiques of working arrangements, economic exploitation, and race and class dynamics. The domestic workers with whom I conducted my research frequently experienced significant hardship and injustice. Many lost apartments over the two years in which I knew them. Others shared stories of social isolation and in many cases their sacrifices of years of mothering their own children to work abroad in the United States. Workers' judgments, therefore, not only managed gendered power dynamics but also evaluated the personal or parental shortcomings of their employers, partially alleviating the strain of grossly unequal employment relationships in an unprotected industry.

Complaint at the Department of Labor

May spent nearly an hour describing her past childcare positions, frequently characterizing the children as "having her heart," and reporting that she remained in contact with several of her former wards who were now college students in the tristate area. May had moved to New York from Barbados, where she was born decades earlier. She worked in both childcare and eldercare over her long career, sometimes combining several part-time positions with multiple families. At the time that she and I spoke, May was working seven days per week as an eldercare provider. Of her last full-time childcare employer in Battery Park, she told me, "She's not a parent. She adopted the little boy and she has no knowledge of being a parent. She had four huge cats in the house. And she brought the baby and she does not take care of the baby. A real parent would want to spend time with the kids. Not her." Although, as I soon learned, her employer committed multiple labor law violations and showed a general lack of consideration, including unpaid hours, unpaid overtime, ever-expanding job requirements, and abrupt termination, May's judgment focused on her evident parental failings rather than employment grievances. Visibly distressed by her memories of that position, she relayed in great detail the unkempt state of the apartment, the residual filth of her employer's four oversized felines, and the pain she experienced upon arriving each morning to find the baby crying alone in his urine-soaked sheets with a soiled diaper and "sour" odor. According to May, his mother's explanation—"He did a poop last night, so I didn't think he'd have a poop today"—cemented her criminal inattentiveness. "Every day the baby goes. A baby goes three, four times, as soon as the baby eats food," she explained to me, opening her eyes wide to communicate her incredulity at her employer's lack of parenting skills. After fulminating about the unattended litter boxes, excess cat hair, and feces throughout the apartment, May added, "So she fired me. For no reason, but she fired me."

May's stories resonated with other, though less dramatic, stories I heard from domestic workers throughout New York City—exemplifying how the personalism of domestic work encourages employers and workers to filter disagreements through interpersonal lenses and illustrating how these individual judgments, while effective in the communal setting, as we will see, offer no protection from termination or other forms of employer retaliation. More than a year after her employer fired her, May and I accompanied her pro bono attorney to an informal Department of Labor hearing in downtown Manhattan. May had brought a wage-theft suit against her former employer, who refused to pay her for all of the hours that she had worked. Given the lack of an official timeclock in the employer's private home, the isolated nature of private childcare, and the one-employer-to-one-employee ratio, the department had to make a decision based on May's and the employer's accounts.

The Department of Labor officer had called May into the office to clarify the records she had submitted regarding her overtime hours, as there was a significant discrepancy between May's reported hours and those submitted by her employer. "Can you provide additional evidence of your overtime hours? Or an explanation for why your records vary so greatly from the employer's?" the officer inquired. Guardedly, May assured the officer that she routinely arrived early and remained late, waiting for her employer to arrive home from the bar. She described evenings on which she noticed her employer's car pull into the driveway after work and watched her cross the street to the neighborhood bar, only to finally return home an hour later.

"Do you have evidence of this?" the officer probed, as May detailed the nearly uninhabitable conditions of her employer's apartment, describing with contempt the cat hair on the furniture, the cat feces left on the floor for days at a time, and the chronically unattended infant. Growing impatient, the officer pulled a photocopy of a Post-it note from her thick file. Apparently, at some point during her tenure, May had written the baby's feeding times on this Post-it for her employer, to ensure that she would feed the baby at the appropriate time in the evening. Her employer, however, had submitted it as evidence of hours worked.

May's lawyer attempted to explain discrepancies by prompting her to respond to directed questions. "Did the age of child when you watched him impact the overtime required? Did your boss have a job change that affected the hours recorded?" But May ignored these prompts, instead reiterating accusations of her employer's unacceptable parenting and neglect, and the unceasing addition of non-child-care-related tasks to her workload.

May began getting frustrated and upset in the hearing, but her attorney and the Department of Labor lawyer continued on in dry, legal discourse. Many anthropologists have noticed that legal settings—like court proceedings or depositions—require the presentation of objective facts without any emotional appeals or moral claims (Brown and Halley 2002; Povinelli 2002). They also note that this standard is especially hard to reconcile with accounts that are likely to stir one's emotions, such as stories of sexual violence, or gendered or race-based discrimination and mistreatment (Greenhouse 2008; Mulla 2014). May encountered a similar conundrum in her hearing. She felt strongly about how poorly the employer had treated her, as well as the employer's own child. Yet, when she spoke in those terms—using gender-based judgments and complaints—the officer and May's attorney essentially ignored her. Unable to resolve the overtime discrepancy, the officer explained that they would continue with May's charges of wage theft and unpaid overtime based on another previous employee's records.

May's unsuccessful Department of Labor testimony highlights how in the individual encounter between one worker and one (or two) employers, using emotionally stirring appeals, like complaints, fail because of the embedded power imbalance. But, as we turn to see how DWU activists found one another and shared their grievances, we will also see that the use of complaint in meetings and informal conversations became something much more transformative for the domestic worker movement.

DWU and Collective Complaint

Finding One Another in the Wilderness

Working in a private home means there are no formal workplace rules or laws governing employer or employee conduct. Early in my research, during a DWU meeting of nannies and eldercare providers, a DWU member and full-time nanny explained that care workers' workplaces are "not a firm where there are tons of people's rules and regulations you follow. Every situation is different. Every home is different. Every parent wants something different from you for their children. So how do you structure yourself to be comfortable in this isolation that you're in?" Working in the privacy of an employer's home means that workers not only experience isolation but also, as this DWU member's observation illustrates so well, they often do not have clear policies or human resource departments outlining job duties and expectations. Furthermore, the laws that typically apply in other workplaces—in factories, office buildings, and stores—do not apply in private residences.

This lack of formal labor standards has left the determination of employment terms entirely up to individual employers and domestic workers (and may explain why so many domestic workers link better parenting by their employers with better working conditions in general). As a result, DWU representatives described the industry as a wilderness, both for workers negotiating duties, wages, and hours and for employers trying to ensure quality care in their homes.

DWU's early outreach efforts supplied domestic workers with crucial information about appropriate wages. Early on, Ai-jen Poo, DWU's then lead organizer and founder, distributed flyers that advised nannies, in particular, about the payment they should expect for the level of care they provided. "It was 2000 when I got a flyer from Ai-jen, when they had rates," remembered Evelyn, another nanny and DWU member. I asked her, "They were putting out rates first [before embarking on the Domestic Workers' Bill of Rights campaign]?" She replied, "Rates for [caring for] one baby, how much. One child and room, board, whatever." This outreach gave individual nannies and caregivers the opportunity to compare their own salaries to the norms across New York City, countering some of the isolation of these jobs. These early efforts to uplift domestic work jobs share similarities with how other domestic workers have relied on their social networks and worker organizations to improve their individual work experiences. For example, in their research among domestic workers in Oakland's Chinatown, sociologists Cynthia Cranford and Jennifer Chun (2017) note that workers even established and circulated a list of unfavorable employers to warn and protect other workers.

While domestic workers labor alone inside private homes, cleaning and caring for old and young, many childcare providers' work also takes them to parks, libraries, and playgrounds where they can connect with other care workers. Brown (2011, 41) notes, in fact, that her research focus shifted from an exploration of the isolation childcare providers experienced in their workplaces to a study of how "childcare providers created community through the use of public places." DWU activists and allies built on this existing use of public places by childcare providers to recruit new members to meetings. Many longtime members trace their DWU activity back to a park or playground interaction.

Often—as was the case for Meva—the women I spoke with had advocated for themselves and fellow domestic workers on their own before realizing that a collective organization existed. Meva was a nanny and preschool teacher, and a newer member of DWU at the time of my research. She quickly became quite active in the organization, joining its many committees, and eventually becoming a member of the board. Meva had grown up in Guatemala, where she was a preschool teacher; traveled to France and Ireland as an au pair; and then moved to New York in 2005 to pursue training in early childhood education. "I love to teach," she told me. Meva began independently recruiting Latina nannies prior to joining DWU:

I was sitting in the park in summer of 2010 with my friends, all Latino people, and we all were complaining about the bad treatment. I was like, "Ok, we cannot be just sitting here and complaining. Let's organize and do something." I started by creating a web page or something, like to organize Latino nannies. Then through one of my friends who liked DWU [on Facebook], I was like, "Hmm, that sounds familiar. That sounds like the thing I want to do." That was a Monday and on Saturday I went to the general meeting and I was like, "Ok, this is what I was looking for. I don't have to organize anything else. This is what I wanted."

Evelyn shared a similar story. Other nannies had "always come to ask me questions," she explained, "So I'm always looking out for people. You know, this is who I was." But Evelyn explained that due to her busy work schedule, "I didn't know that there was an organization because I had so much work. So, when this flyer came to me from Ai-jen, I was glad." For many eldercare and childcare providers, demanding work schedules and long daily commutes to and from their place of employment—on top of their own family obligations—made it difficult to join DWU and attend regular meetings. This was certainly the case for Evelyn, as it was a number of weeks before she could finally attend a meeting. While most New York City care workers were not an active part of DWU or their sister organizations, DWU members' activism supported care workers across the city, even when they themselves could not participate in the group.

Building an Emotional Community

Following a DWU meeting one Saturday afternoon, Sharon, a long-time DWU board member who had worked as a nanny, housecleaner, and elder companion over her decades-long career, pulled a folding chair toward us as we discussed household employers' expectations. She climbed up onto the chair, while continuing to tell me about the demanding cleaning tasks she'd been asked to do. Teetering on the edge of the chair, with one arm stretched up toward the wall in front of her and the other on my shoulder to steady herself, she panto-mimed the act of cleaning ceilings, moldings, fans, and ledges, before hopping down and exclaiming that the employer who made this request would never consider climbing and bending to perform those tasks. "They think they can ask *us* to do these things, you understand?" she asked me. Her critique of employer expectations was expressed through an embodied reenactment of how physically demanding, difficult, and dangerous such tasks are.

Sharon's re-enactment vividly illustrated for me that the determination of job duties was a chief and recurrent source of complaint for in-home workers. The persistent, underlying question, "Who is in control of how a worker performs her job?" points to the tension between care workers and their employers. According to the women I spoke with, the type and extent of cleaning responsibilities varied with the job role. Typically, nannies agreed that cleaning and straightening up the children's areas, taking care of the baby's laundry and food preparation, and also doing some basic kitchen chores were all part of their caretaking labor. The personalism in domestic work settings encouraged workers to indirectly manipulate their work arrangements and their employers (as far as they were able) as a means of managing their caregiving and cleaning labor. Domestic workers delicately complained to their employers, hoping to lessen their workloads and avoid termination. Given the isolated nature of the worksites, DWU meetings and informal conversations gave care workers a space to collectively condemn what they regarded as unfair labor extraction.

Commiserating around DWU's conference table, tired and sweaty from a marathon training that spanned one of the warmest weekends in July 2012, Meva shared her recent experience with a parent who sought to add shopping to her childcare duties. "Do you do groceries?" her employer inquired. "I answered, well, which one do you want first? The babies or the groceries? Which one do you want me to do first? Because I can't do both," she proclaimed to a room full of fellow care workers. Another DWU member agreed, by asking an imaginary parent, "What matters to you?" In attempting to refuse additional non-caretaking duties, nannies may intimate that employers' other demands compromise appropriate and safe childcare. Resisting being assigned additional cleaning, shopping, pet sitting, and extra childcare tasks was one way care workers tried to maintain a manageable workload.

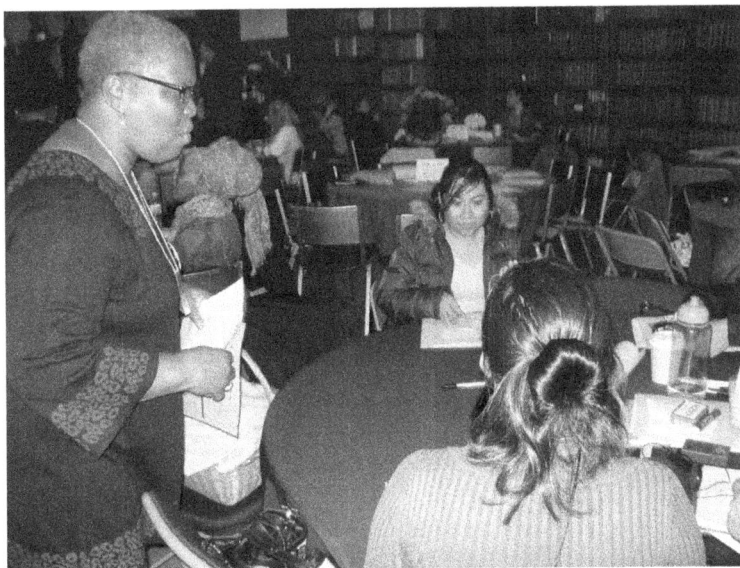

Figure 1.1 DWU board members and members strategize during a citywide convention.

DWU members used their meetings to instruct one another in effective responses to employers' requests, including by restating employment tasks in terms of parental priorities. At another DWU meeting, longtime DWU member Carol described a recent negotiation of job duties as a combination of direct discussion and subtle management of her female employer: "The mother would sit with that baby all day long, and then she started designating stuff. I said to her: 'Well, I'm a babysitter; I'm not a housekeeper.' She had this long list: including cleaning the baseboard around the house. I said, 'Do you clean the baseboard?' She said, 'Yes.' So I said, 'Whenever you are cleaning the baseboard, I will assist you.'" Carol's boldness ("I'm a babysitter, not a housekeeper") set an example for the other DWU members present. Carol explained her tactic, "Indirectly, I was saying to her, 'I'm not going to do this.' So, I watched her baby." Through years of DWU organizing and rehearsing assertiveness among allies, Carol established a clear yet subtle strategy to maintain control over her labor, evincing childcare's highly personal and idiosyncratic aspects.

These collective complaints established commonality and a sense of shared circumstances among domestic workers that were otherwise prevented by their isolated workplaces, an example of what anthropologist Myriam Jimeno (2007) calls "emotional community." The emotional community creates a "political bond," legitimating members' grievances and buoying their ongoing activism (Macleod and De Marinis 2018, 5). Sharing negotiation strategies, as Carol and Meva did, helped other domestic workers improve their own working conditions to the extent they were able because they offered the language to negotiate additional duties with employers.

Collective Complaint as a Basis for Solidarity

Through conversations and performative complaints, like the enactment of cleaning a ceiling fan, DWU meetings allowed care workers to critique their working conditions through collective complaint. Those moments make it easier to envision the possibility for collective action outside of the circumscribed meeting space. Sociologist Rhacel Salazar Parreñas (2001, 194) argues that the tactics of individual workers, such as managing the assignment of additional tasks through indirect avoidance or judgment, "are in fact collective acts"; she writes, "They do not reside at the level of the individual but are rooted in the collective consciousness of a shared struggle among domestic workers." In DWU meetings and events, storytelling, performance, and conversation drew out and highlighted the collectivity of these acts. Katherine's performance from the Preface, in which she read out a job description in the form of a poem, for example, actively cultivated communal sentiment.

Performance has been a key avenue for DWU's collectivization of complaint. Performances like Katherine's amplified and validated individual worker frustrations and complaints, and simultaneously shaped the linguistic forms that those expressions of discontent might take. As Madison (2010, 224) argues, "Performance and activism are mutually constitutive. . . . Abstract moral arguments and political theory are unveiled in action and their consequences made more apparent through the body and embodied interpretations of daily life." Katherine's performance—appropriating an otherwise unremarkable employment advertisement to highlight and collectivize the indignities that care workers routinely experience and for which they have limited individual recourse—unveiled, as Madison argues, the moral arguments and politics that buoy DWU's solidarity activism. By removing the job posting from its intended context (an online nanny job board) and irreverently enacting it for us, Katherine invoked what Madison (2010, 6) describes as the "shared naming and marking of injustice" realized through public performance.

Communal settings provide an occasion to collectively experience, express, and object to not only asymmetrical working conditions but also the broader global processes that facilitate them. Based on her research among home healthcare providers, anthropologist Maria de la Luz Ibarra (2013, 78) argues that "caring for an elderly ward is about creating a more just world, of critiquing through deeds the inequality of globalization that makes human intimacy so difficult." Ibarra's observation suggests that, through their work caring for others, domestic workers embody and enact visions of justice that challenge the precarity of globalization. I view New York City nannies' judgments of their employers as sharing many parallels with the labor of Ibarra's eldercare providers, who "critiqu[e] through deeds the inequality of globalization" (78). Through performances and poems, complaining and strategizing, nannies criticized the priorities of middle- and upper-class families in a city characterized by remarkable wealth disparity and the extensive commercialization of otherwise-unremunerated caregiving exchanges (Sassen 1991). For members of DWU, this vision of justice was also intentionally enacted together through their solidarity organizing at meetings, events, and protests.

The persistence of nannies' individual judgments and their experiences of workplace vulnerability, abrupt termination, and inconsiderate employers suggests that the construction of women's natural role as caretakers undermines the notion that care work is legitimate work. Anti-immigrant policy, legacies of race-based oppression, and ongoing racial discrimination further disadvantage care workers. The growing number of workers with casual, dispersed, and non-unionized jobs indicates that the problems of precarity extend beyond the caregiver sector, gesturing toward a potential reality for workers across industries.

Collective complaint united dispersed domestic workers for decades as they challenged the broader national antilabor tide to introduce a new labor law and to fight for their collective dignity on the job. Unlike Jewel's hiring frustrations, Danata's frequent and abrupt terminations, or May's Department of Labor difficulties, the indictment of parental priorities and excesses represented in Katherine's performance took place alongside broader critiques of structural inequality, neoliberal globalization, and resulting insecurity and displacement. Thus, collective complaint has fueled the organization's broader political claims by establishing common ground among caregivers. Establishing shared estimations of caregivers' employers and, in so doing, proclaiming their collective political priorities offered DWU members a route to overcome other salient differences, such as race, nationality, immigration status, and language in their efforts to uplift and improve care-sector jobs. In the next chapter, I describe the political education trainings that I participated in with DWU members to offer a sense of how DWU evolved from an emotional community to a political force through its deep engagement with history.

---

*Portions of Chapter 1 previously appeared in Alana Glaser, "Collective Complaint: New York City Care Workers' Community, Performance, and the Limits of Labor Law," *PoLAR: Political and Legal Anthropology Review* 43, no. 2 (2020): 195–210. https://doi.org/10.1111/plar.12377.

2

"The Work That Makes
All Other Work Possible"

DWU's Political Education

One afternoon in 2011, as part of a Domestic Work Histories workshop conducted by Domestic Workers United at a national conference, I stood at the front of a brightly lit, carpeted hotel conference room with a group of five other women from across the country, reading from a handout provided to me by workshop leaders earlier in the afternoon:

> I am a Negro woman, and I was born and reared in the South. Since I was ten years old, I have been a servant in one capacity or another for White families. More than two thirds of the Negroes of the town where I live are menial servants of one kind or another, and besides that, more than two thirds of the Negro women here, whether married or single, are compelled to work for a living as nurses, cooks, washerwomen, chambermaids, seamstresses, hucksters, janitresses, and the like.

I pantomimed removing laundry from a clothing line and folding it.

Then, Inez, another woman from my group, stood up from her nearby chair and read from her handout. "I frequently work sixteen hours a day. I'm compelled by my contract, which is oral only, to sleep in the house. I don't know what it is to go to church. I don't know what it is to go to a lecture or entertainment of any kind. I live a treadmill life," she said, as she approached me and placed her hand on my shoulder in a gesture of empathy and understanding. Two other women from our group rose from their chairs and knelt just to the side of our conference room stage, pretending to be children crossing the street. Inez and I reached for them, as they passed without acknowledgment. "I see my own children only when they happen to see me on the streets," she read.

We all returned to our seats while Laura, another member of our group, summarized our skit for the audience of domestic work activists gathered from around the country. Our group had been assigned a fictionalized first-person account of a "free colored woman" working in the U.S. South as a domestic worker. We were instructed to act out her account in whatever way we envisioned and to perform it for the larger group. In turn, other groups depicted different scenarios from earlier and later time periods, all written by the workshop leaders based on historical biographies and research.

During our planning conversations earlier in the afternoon, all of our group members—domestic workers from Texas, Chicago, Georgia, Massachusetts, and New York, all affiliated with various workers' rights organizations—pinpointed the painful separation of parent and child as the emotional crux of the first-person account we were assigned. We therefore crafted our short skit to dramatize the pain of maternal separation experienced by domestic workers throughout history and today. I found the exercise to be profoundly educational and moving. For other members of my group, particularly those women who lived apart from their own children while caring and cleaning in someone else's home, it was especially resonant.

Many DWU meetings and workshops used performance to explain historical precursors and social-scientific aspects of contemporary care work. Often, these tactics were met with some hesitancy. At the Domestic Work Histories workshop, for example, the facilitator told us that our acting skills would be on display, asking, "Are we ready for today?" to which the room replied with a resounding and hearty, "No," followed by laughter and chatter. But, for most of us, our initial reluctance and nervousness about performing a skit eventually gave way to a feeling of connection to the people whose stories

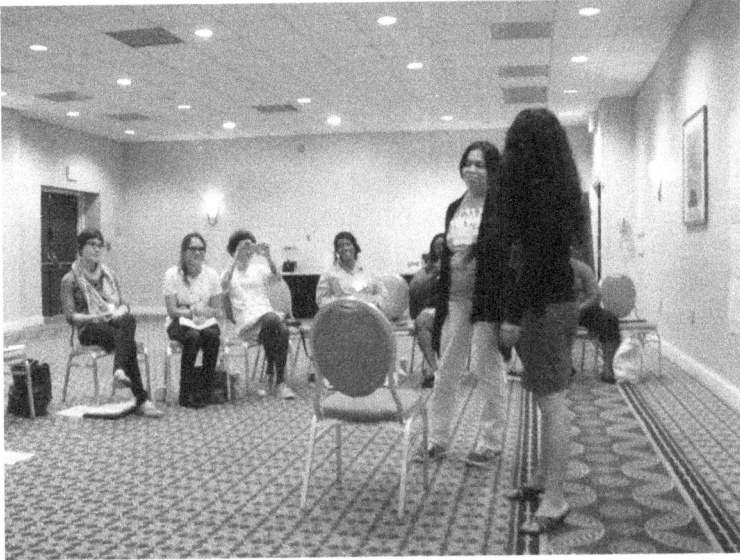

Figure 2.1 Domestic work activists act out biographies of domestic workers throughout history.

we enacted and read and for one another, as we told our own stories sparked by the content of the historical accounts.

Through their campaign slogans, education events, flyers, teach-ins, and online social media and website content, DWU provided deeper context that domestic worker activists relied on to build a shared sense of purpose, both with one another and with allies in other organizations. Often, as we saw in this daylong training, the curriculum was interactive, depicting through personal narrative, performance, and lecture how slavery, indentured servitude, and immigration policies all shape the provision of domestic labor. Edu-cators frequently began by describing the legacies of slavery and cen-turies of codified white supremacy that continue to influence this sector. Trainings not only provided historical context for the working conditions described in the previous chapter but also allowed domes-tic workers the opportunity to place their own experiences in relation to that history, as they simultaneously considered and empathized with the experiences of others living at different points in time and in various parts of the world. These histories have also influenced how society values domestic work, how employers remunerate it, and how legislators conceive of rights for workers in these sectors—all implications highlighted at DWU trainings. These engaging historical and political trainings combined with shared workplace strategies served as crucial connective tissue, transforming the emotional community generated by workers into a political force demanding structural change at local, state, federal, and international levels.

In this chapter, I ground my retelling of the history of domestic work in the United States in DWU's educational practices, alternating between a bird's-eye overview and moments from DWU training events designed to educate members on this history. By describing trainings that I attended and discussed with domestic workers, I capture the organization's political education tactics, arguing that these practices form the backbone of DWU's political strength and solidarity. Additionally, this chapter outlines the history of domestic work in the United States while introducing key scholarly ideas about this type of work and the people who do it. This background sets the context for why legal protections for this sector did not exist until 2010 in the United States. In short, in addition to describing some of DWU's educational approaches, I fill in historical details affecting their current working conditions as well.

Historicizing the Work That Makes All Other Work Possible

DWU members frequently say that "domestic work is the work that makes all other work possible" or a variation thereof. For example, during the campaign to pass the Domestic Workers' Bill of Rights, they rallied support with the slogan "Respect the Work that Makes All Other Work Possible," as depicted on the banner carried by three DWU members on the cover of this book. What they mean is that working families can go to their day jobs (as doctors, bus drivers, bankers, etcetera) trusting that the person in whose care they have left their child, home, or relative will provide adequate and reliable nurturance and protection. This DWU slogan encapsulates the function of what social scientists refer to as *reproductive labor*.

Reproductive labor is "the physical and social, daily and generational reproduction of the labor force" (Gimenez 1990, 26). In their research on ride-hailing applications, gender studies scholars Julietta Hua and Kasturi Ray (2021, 5) define *reproductive labor* a bit more expansively: "exertions enabling the flourishing of another's life, the tending of the body, home, and well-being of another (and thus the nation) that is often demonetized and generally undervalued because such work is constructed as natural and expected." The concept of reproductive labor has roots in the early political-economic theory of *productive labor* discussed by scholars like Adam Smith and Karl Marx. Marx ([1867] 1977), in particular, critiqued industrial capitalism's effects on workers, power relations, and the ability of people to meet basic needs for food, shelter, warmth, and so on. Workers who toiled in European factories for low wages and long hours were involved in productive labor, Marx reasoned, because their effort produced *surplus value*, generating profits claimed by the factory owner. An owner puts in machines, raw materials, and wages for workers. Workers put in their time, strength, and skill to transform raw materials into goods that owners can sell. The difference between the amount that an owner pays workers in wages and the amount the owner sells the goods for is the profit. So, Marx argued, this type of labor produces profits—or surplus value—and is, therefore, *productive*.

Reproductive labor refers to all of the activities required to ensure that workers as individuals, and society as an entity, continue to exist day after day and generation after generation (Laslett and Brenner 1989, 383). Unlike productive labor, reproductive labor does not typically produce profits.[1] In this way, reproductive labor's value is hidden. Yet, it is necessary for the maintenance—or reproduction—of society.

Someone must care for children, prepare meals, clean homes, attend to the sick, assist elderly people, and generally keep society running. Sociologist Saskia Sassen (1991) has demonstrated that large, global cities and international finance centers, like New York City, function as well as they do only because of the reproductive labor that nannies, food vendors, janitors, building attendants, cleaners, trash collectors, taxi drivers, restaurant workers, and other lower paid workers provide. By ensuring that homes, offices, and city streets are clean; by preparing and providing food; by caring for the old and young; and by maintaining all of the city's residential buildings and workplaces, these workers keep the city running day after day and generation after generation. But their labor does not necessarily produce profits (although in some cases, the labor of personal chefs and home health aides will produce profits for the companies employing them).

A longtime DWU member and full-time nanny explained reproductive labor to me this way: "When you really think about it, when I go into work in the morning, I allow my employers to go to work. I allow them to have a social life. I allow them to function like normal citizens in society without having to worry about the care of their child, or worry about daycare, or worry about any of that." She added, "That's a huge undertaking." Her explanation illustrates the relationship between reproductive labor and productive labor. During the early phase of the COVID-19 global pandemic, most reproductive labor assumed the new moniker of "essential work," reflecting the indispensable role of reproductive laborers in society. Unlike jobs in, say, advertising or finance, those working in fields that society relies on day to day could not shelter at home. Without reproductive labor, there would be no workers to labor for profits in the productive sector. This is why, as DWU members so often say, "domestic work is the work that makes all other work possible."

Who Does Reproductive Labor?

Reproductive labor can be accomplished by any combination of people in any number of ways. As sociologist Mignon Duffy (2007, 320) explains, "Work can be done by family members or volunteers for no pay; workers can come into employers' homes to cook, clean, and care for children or ill family members; or reproductive labor can be performed in institutions such as hospitals, restaurants, childcare centers, and nursing homes." Yet, in the United States, reproductive labor inside private homes is often thought of as women's work. Scholars characterize this phenomenon as the *gendered division of labor*, referring to the organization of tasks based on gender roles. In her foundational study of domestic work in the United States, sociologist Mary Romero (1992, 17) describes the romanticized notion of a gendered division of household labor, characterized by "smiling mothers wearing aprons [who] place delicious meals on the dining room table, [while] husbands carry the trash to the curb once a week." Many in the United States and elsewhere regard this division of labor as somehow natural or normal—even if a bit outdated.

In contrast, anthropologists have documented how the tasks associated with reproductive labor range in their organization and distribution across the world (Mead 1935; Oakley 1972). Archeologists have described Ice Age societies in which everyone—from grandparents to infants strapped across their parents' backs—likely participated in communal hunting with nets to provision food for grand feasts (Adovasio, Soffer, and Page 2007). Anthropologist Agnes Estioko-Griffin (1986) similarly found that women, not men, hunt in groups in some Filipino communities. Anthropologist Margaret Mead (1935) famously documented societies, like the Tchambuli society in Papua New Guinea, in which childrearing and homemaking were men's responsibilities. She also studied societies such as the Arapesh in Papua New Guinea, in which all adults shared caretaking, cleaning, and cooking equally, without regard for gender. Anthropologist Barry Hewlett (1993) has studied a group called the Aka, living in the Central African Republic, where fathers play primary roles in nurturance and infant care. In my own Brooklyn neighborhood, the sight of young men pushing strollers or walking with infants bundled tightly to their chests is increasingly common, as newer generations of fathers share in childcare tasks that once might have been relegated exclusively to women.

Since such variety and flexibility exists, why do many people in the United States[2] consider domestic labor "women's work"? Feminist theorists Mariarosa Dalla Costa and Selma James (1972, 46) incisively note that "domestic labor is not essentially 'feminine work'; a woman does not work less or get less exhausted than a man from washing and cleaning." By tracing the historical origins of a particular social arrangement—the gendered division of household labor, for example—DWU members and other scholars engage in the intellectual process of *historicizing* a given social arrangement. When scholars historicize a concept, practice, or belief, they explain the processes by which certain circumstances arose, separating it from its apparent, taken-for-granted naturalness. Often this type of intellectual activity is, in and of itself, a political action. To argue, for example, that there isn't any natural or universal basis to existing gendered divisions of labor—rather they arose due to specific historical circumstances—is to imply that these divisions are malleable.

DWU trainings enact this process as they outline the history of domestic work in the United States and the various groups of people who were responsible for it. For example, when discussing the evolution of U.S. labor laws, DWU's director, speaking in Spanish, asked the class (all of whom wore headsets to facilitate real-time translation from Spanish to English), "Who performed household work in the early history of the United States?" With this question, the director was prompting the participants to think of the labor of enslaved and indentured people across the United States. The legacy of U.S. slavery is particularly relevant to DWU's political analysis and education since it shapes domestic work's longstanding legal exclusion from basic protections such as minimum wage laws.

U.S. Slavery in the Sixteenth and Seventeenth Centuries

The morning of the Domestic Work Histories workshop, the trainer welcomed us and asked us to form groups of four, each of which would be given a case study. I joined one of two English-speaking groups. There was one Spanish-speaking group and a bilingual group as well. After distributing fictionalized first-person accounts from women performing domestic work across history and place, and explaining the day's plan, the trainer said:

> We're going to develop an understanding of the broad historical development of the domestic worker industry and the relationship to slavery. We're also going to discuss the ways that industry has changed and how it has also stayed the same. We're also going to talk about the connection between the history of domestic work and our experiences with the work today.

After a bit of brainstorming about what we knew of domestic work conditions in early American history, the trainer described the origins of U.S. slavery in broad terms:

> In the South, European settlers built huge cotton plantations and tobacco plantations. That was what was going on at the time. Thousands of people were stolen from Africa to work on these plantations. Like many of you said, these slaves were working in very abusive and brutal conditions. They were working with severe violence and overtime, as we can imag-

ine, because maybe they had no time to begin work and no time to end work. It was whenever the master said you had to work, that's what had to happen. Enslaved women in this time period were abused in many ways.

Slavery in the Americas "was a political and economic system in which a group of whites extracted as much labor as possible from blacks . . . through threat or use of force" (Jones 1985, 13). But it was more than simply an economic or political arrangement: it was a dehumanizing system of oppression and coercion that introduced a racial hierarchy, established denigrating racial ideologies, and enforced racial terror against people of African descent in the Americas. Our trainer then prodded us:

> Of course there was domestic work back then, right? Somebody needed to clean the house for the master. Oftentimes, these women worked, and they were not given the opportunity to even raise their own kids, because they were on the plantation taking care of the master, his wife, and his children, while the children of the slaves were oftentimes sold into other plantations to work. So, there's the division of family that's also happening within this time period. A lot of the slaves, when they weren't cleaning the house, they were in the cotton fields picking cotton . . . cleaning from sunup until sundown.

Domestic work inside the home was the "major occupation" for both enslaved men and women across the United States, according to Romero (1992, 73). Depending on the region, enslaved men and women's agricultural labor also produced cotton, rice, and tobacco, enriching White colonists and establishing the United States' worldwide economic prominence. "In addition to working the fields," states a report authored by Domestic Workers United and DataCenter (2006, 11) titled *Home Is Where the Work Is*, "slaves were required to perform the household work that sustained plantation life: spinning thread and weaving fabric, cooking and serving meals, washing dishes and clothes, cleaning homes, and nurturing their masters' children. Slaves endured long work hours, and they frequently experienced physical and sexual abuse at the hands of their masters."

DWU's political education and activism focus on the effects of slavery's legacy for contemporary care workers in the United States. One of the central points that this trainer and others made is that the institution of slavery was itself instrumental in creating the divisions among people that what we now call "race." As our trainer explained:

> At first, the African slaves worked alongside the European slaves, so it wasn't a separation. They were all slaves together, working together. But the master then thought of this—this—this terminology called "indentured servitude," which meant that the European slaves, because they were White, were treated better than the Black slaves who were from African descent. They were given a little bit more privileges than that of the Black slaves. They were given land and guns. This began to cause, as you can imagine, some sort of animosity and hatred between both groups of slaves. At this time, the European slaves and the African slaves didn't see themselves as equal, because by the masters' say-so, they were divided, and their conditions of living show that there was a separation.

Indeed, during the seventeenth century, British colonists indentured laborers from Britain and Ireland as well as Native Americans and Africans to work in tobacco fields in the Chesapeake Bay colonies (Jones 1985, 11). In those arrangements, indentured servants had some leisure time and could expect to leave their roles after a set period of time. Anthropologist Audrey Smedley (2007a) recounts a 1670s uprising in which hundreds of African, Native American, and European laborers confronted the colonies' political and economic elite, arguing that indentured servants and even poor free laborers presented a unified threat to British colonial rule. To prevent such insubordination, she explains, the colonists introduced a series of laws that singled out Africans and their descendants, curtailing their rights and movement and "imposing a condition of permanent slavery on them" (4). They also created a new category:

> They began to homogenize all Europeans, regardless of ethnicity, status, or social class, into a new category. The first time the term "White," rather than "Christian" or their ethnic names

(English, Irish, Scots, Portuguese, German, Spanish, Swede) appeared in the public record was seen in a law passed in 1691 that prohibited the marriage of Europeans with Negroes, Indians, and mulattoes (Smedley 2007b, 118). A clearly separated category of Negroes as slaves allowed newly freed European servants opportunities to realize their ambitions and to identify common interests with the wealthy and powerful. Laws were passed offering material advantages and social privileges to poor whites. In this way, colony leaders consciously contrived a social control mechanism to prevent the unification of the working poor (Allen 1997). Physical features became markers of racial (social) status. (Smedley 2007a, 6)

Thus, "slavery became clearly racialized, limited to blacks and Native Americans," as historian Evelyn Nakano Glenn (2012, 26) argues. Sociologists have defined *racialization* as "the extension of racial meaning to a previously racially unclassified relationship, social practice, or group" (Omi and Winant [1986] 2015, 111). As we will see, the codification of racial difference and discrimination enacted through the racialization of slavery shaped the domestic work industry differently across regions and had ongoing impacts well after slavery's official end.

The British entered the transatlantic slave trade in 1672; by the middle of the eighteenth century, kidnapping, enslavement, forced labor, and violent oppression of Africans and their descendants had supplanted other labor arrangements in the southern regions of the United States. The strenuous demands of cotton cultivation and the invention of the cotton gin in 1791 propelled the inhumane system of domination in the South. By 1830, the U.S. system of slavery had become entrenched through cotton plantations in the South and textile mills in the North. Because the U.S. system of slavery was embedded both economically and societally, its influence over the lives of enslaved Africans and their descendants has had profound implications that extend to contemporary domestic work relationships. Sociologist Judith Rollins (1985, 212), for example, has historicized how the dehumanization of twentieth-century domestic workers was enacted through employers' social and linguistic practices originating in the context of slavery.

Immigration to the North during the 1800s

During this period, indentured servitude offered European immigrants opportunities to work off their financial obligations. Irish immigration to the Eastern United States, which began in the 1820s, intensified in the 1840s due to the Irish Potato Famine, and then steadily continued through the later part of the century, deeply influenced the character and perception of domestic labor in the urban North. Historian Faye Dudden (1983, 60) writes that, following the Irish Potato Famine, "it began to look as though every servant was Irish, at least in the major seaboard cities. . . . The Irish 'biddy' became the stereotype of the servant, and Biddy jokes celebrated her inadequacies. Biddy answered the door by yelling through the keyhole; Biddy, accustomed to descending by a ladder, went downstairs backwards." Middle- and upper-class women formed national organizations to facilitate the movement of working-class and poor women to Western states as servants ("help"), including the Protective Emigrant Organization, the American Emigrant Company, and the Irish Emigration Fund (Sutherland 1981, 16).

In sharp contrast to the experiences of enslaved Africans in the U.S. South, Irish workers gained immediate access to both housing and wages through household employment. Steady wages permitted Irish domestic workers to reliably remit the bulk of their earnings to their families abroad, either to assist in bringing additional kin to the United States or to aid the "family economies left behind in ruins" (Dudden 1983, 61; see also di Leonardo 1998, 105). Comparing the dehumanizing oppression of enslaved Africans who worked in domestic roles with the relative freedom and mobility of immigrant Irish domestic workers highlights the ongoing impact of slavery on this sector, even during a period when most domestic workers were "White" immigrants.

DWU's training captured the geographical specificity and complexity of the different histories of domestic work in the United States. Enacting another script during our training, we next performed a passage from a fictionalized first-hand account of an Irish immigrant, taking turns to carefully sound out the tricky dialect. I began: "What did we eat? Well, just potatoes. On Sundays, once a month, we'd maybe have a bit of flitch [a potato-based jelly roll]. When the potatoes rotted, that was the hard times. . . . One of the twins died the famine year of the typhus and, well, she sickened of the herbs and roots we eat. We had no potatoes." Inez followed, reading about the woman's travel to the United States:

The ship was a sailin' vessel, the *Mary Jane*. The passage was $12. You brought your own eatin', your tea an' meal, an' most had flitch. The steerage was a dirty place and we were eight weeks on the voyage, over time three weeks. The food ran scarce, I tell you, but the captain gave some to us, and them that had plenty was kind to the others. I've heard bad stories of things that went on in the steerage in them old times—small-pox and fevers and starvation and worse, but I saw nothing of them in my ship. When I get here, Mrs. Bent let Tilly keep me for two months to teach me, me being such a greenhorn. I got $2 'til I learned to cook good, and then $3 and then $4. I was in that house as cook and nurse for twenty-two years.

Other members of my group continued reading from this first-person account highlighting the independence and economic advancement—even if meager—that this fictionalized Irish immigrant enjoyed. Through these performances, we became aware of the stark contrast between the experiences of a free Black woman and an Irish immigrant, differences in freedom, autonomy, safety, movement, and ability to earn and save wages.

Something Other Than Work? Victorian-Era Domesticity and Racial Divisions of Reproductive Labor

Meanwhile, changes that occurred during this same time period would cement the popular idea of household labor as women's work. Scholars tend to refer to these changes as the *formation of the domestic sphere* in U.S history (di Leonardo 1991; Rosaldo and Lamphere 1974). In the early nineteenth-century United States, the idea of a "home"—meaning a domain of family life separate from work—did not even exist. Instead, the home was a site of all forms of labor:

farming, weaving, processing crops and livestock for meals, cooking, cleaning, laundry, and caring for young and old. Almost all activities for life took place inside the home or on its property. Anthropologist Jane Collins (1990, 3) argues that the movement of productive activity out of the home in later decades "made it possible, for the first time, to speak of women who labored for their families as 'not working,' or cultivating a home garden as a 'leisure time' activity." In other words, it was not until industrialization moved wage earners outside of the home that the labor associated with caring for families, tending to land and animals, sewing clothing, cleaning, farming family plots, and preparing food stopped being thought of as work.

Toward the middle of the nineteenth century, this arrangement shifted in Northern U.S. cities. Rapid industrialization and growing urbanization accompanied ideological and even spiritual or religious shifts about the very meaning of *home*. Productive labor now occurred outside the home in, for example, textile mills. The home became the site of reproductive labor and only reproductive labor. And for the first time, a strict separation between the external market-driven world and the imagined internal serenity of the domestic space emerged (Dudden 1983, 47). Newly urban middle and entrepreneurial classes reconstructed the domicile, dividing the private home from the professional workplace.

At that time, politicians, religious leaders, and the press gave new meanings to *home* and *housework*, ushering in the nineteenth-century notion of moral motherhood. Dudden (1983, 47) writes, "The ideologues of domesticity began in the popular presses to insist that this physical space corresponded to a separate women's sphere, an area of spiritual comfort." Religious leaders, politicians, journalists, and reformers insisted that White, affluent women belonged indoors, introducing the role of homemaker as the "angel in the home" (Moghari 2020, 51). Along with this new definition of the home and women's place in it, popular presses insisted on "the removal of women and children from the industrial workforce" (Collins 1990, 19). In fact, poor White women and children typically predominated in factories until Progressive era reformers campaigned to remove them from factory work in the North (19). During this era, reformers sought to instruct working-class women to perform "gender-assigned duties and obligations" inside the household, rather than take work in a mill or shop (Glenn 2012, 43).

The development of this separation of home and work instilled the misconception that household labor is "something other than employment"—a spiritual service, a moral obligation, or a womanly duty—that it is, essentially, nonwork (Hondagneu-Sotelo 2001). One longtime DWU board member told me:

> You're at home caring for the kids and cleaning the house and caring for the elderly parents. We oftentimes don't get a "thank you" because it's work that we as women "have" to do. It's in our "caring nature." And I beg to differ. I beg to differ completely. These workers are real workers with real families, real lives, and this is a real industry that needs to be protected, it needs to be uplifted, and it needs to be treated with respect and dignity.

In this critique, the board member excoriates both the gendered division of labor that has naturalized domestic work as nonlabor and draws attention back to the split between productive and reproductive activity that has devalued reproductive work. "I beg to differ completely," she says, rejecting the taken-for-granted naturalness of these historical developments.

Explaining the emergence of a domestic sphere in the Victorian era (1830s–1900), our Domestic Work Histories workshop trainer said, "Wives were seen as the ladies of the house, and it was okay because their role was dignified. Whereas for the slaves and servants who did this work, this work was seen as undignified work. Does that kind of sound familiar in the context of our work that we're doing today?" Researchers have similarly argued that the Victorian-era notion of a domestic sphere recast the idea of domestic labor as somehow undignified. In her formative study of household labor, Glenn (1992) introduces the phrase "the racial division of reproductive labor" to describe the persistent relegation of caregiving and cleaning tasks to women of color and immigrant women into the present. She also observes that affluent White women could claim moral superiority and delicate constitutions because they hired impoverished immigrant women and women of other races to maintain the home, tracing this separation of physical maintenance and spiritual control to that same Victorian-era division of home and workplace.

The notion of the domestic sphere in U.S. history applied narrowly to a thin stratum of wealthy, White women, who in this configuration lessened their own household labor by "hiring out" to young, urban women desperate for employment. In so doing, homemakers further elevated their own status and inscribed the division between the spiritual mastery of the domicile and the physical labor required for its upkeep. The physical labor required to maintain a serene home was indeed significant. The later part of the nineteenth-century "witnessed a larger proportional increase in the number of servants than any other time in American history" (Sutherland 1981, 14). During this period, half of all working women were employed in domestic service, according to the 1870 census (Gimenez 1990, 38).

Following the official end of slavery in 1865, African Americans in the United States continued to experience oppression and exploitation in the White-dominated South and across the country. Debt arrangements prevented African Americans from farming their own land and forced them into situations that closely resembled the forced agricultural labor of the antebellum period (Glenn 2012, 31). Under vagrancy laws, local police could apprehend "idlers"—African Americans who were simply going about their daily lives—and impose fines on them, which they then had to work off through fieldwork, construction, or household service (32). Glenn notes that Black women were especially targeted by these vagrancy laws due to a shortage of domestic workers following emancipation.

The portion of the first-person account that I recited during DWU's Domestic Work Histories training gave us a picture of what happened to African American women under such vagrancy laws: "More than two thirds of the Negro women here, whether married or single, are compelled to work for a living as nurses, cooks, washerwomen, chambermaids, seamstresses, hucksters, janitresses, and the like." The script continued on to mention the vagrancy laws specifically:

> The truth is, we have to work for little or nothing or become vagrants. And that, of course, in this state would mean that we would be arrested, tried and dispatched to the state farm,

where we would surely have to work for nothing or be beaten with many stripes.

Unlike married White women who were encouraged to leave the industrial workforce to be "angels in the home," married Black women had to work outside their homes for meager wages or face arrest (Glenn 2012, 32). DWU trainings invited us to reflect on these long-standing patterns of oppression and racialization by reciting these historical facts in the first-person, using our bodies and our collective voice to retell histories that have shaped domestic work.

Changing Demography of Domestic Work in the Twentieth Century

In the early twentieth century, two factors led to a demographic shift in the profile of domestic workers throughout the United States, making domestic work the chief employment for Black women (Gimenez 1990, 39). The first change was the introduction of immigration restrictions. By the time that the nation geared up for World War I, isolationism bolstered anti-immigration sentiment and xenophobia toward immigrant domestic workers (Coble 2006, 32). World War I also halted the migration of European women—a group that had previously worked in domestic jobs—to the United States (Coble 2006, 35; Palmer 1989, xiii). Immigration laws adopted in 1921 and 1924 drastically "curtailed any post-war resumption of immigration" (Palmer 1989, xiii). These restrictions reduced the numbers of single, White Europeans working as domestic laborers.

During this same period, many emancipated African American women from the South moved to the North, but racist hiring prohibitions prevented them from entering many industries (Coble 2006, 38; Palmer 1989, 67). As a result of restrictions on where they could work, African American women's domestic employment grew by 53 percent during this period (Palmer 1989, 12). They worked as cooks, cleaners, and laundresses in the Northern cities where they moved, pioneering the trend for domestic workers to live apart from the families for whom they worked (Palmer 1989, 68; Rollins 1985, 54). Additionally, the 1927 National Origins Act allowed Caribbean women to migrate to the United States with greater ease, using their respective European colonizers' national quota numbers to gain entrance. These migrant women of African descent frequently found employment in household labor as well, at least on the East Coast, where even now Caribbean women continue to predominate in childcare (Coble 2006, 38).

New Deal Labor Laws

Perhaps the most significant policy changes for workers in the United States came in the 1930s New Deal. *The New Deal* refers to the suite of labor reforms adopted by President Franklin D. Roosevelt in 1935 to mitigate the effects of the Great Depression and to quell growing unrest and rebellion among workers. New Deal laws ensured that most workers received minimum wage and overtime protections. It created social security and unemployment insurance as well, and also supported the formation of labor unions through which workers could band together to demand increases in wages, time off, and even basic things like an eight-hour workday. Beginning in 1933, domestic workers lobbied to be included in New Deal labor, social security, and unemployment protection (Palmer 1989, 71). But, as DWU's Priscilla Gonzalez noted in her tenth anniversary gala welcome letter, these protections excluded domestic work "by name."

During a Nanny Training course, DWU staff educated newly recruited domestic workers on the history of domestic work in the United States, paying special attention to the legal exclusions that have reinforced domestic workers' lack of job protections and low wages for decades. Gonzalez led the training, explaining to the room of more than thirty women that "labor laws in this country were enacted in the 1930s," referring to the New Deal, and continued, "At that time, the group that was doing domestic work were African American women. Not that much time had passed since the time of slavery in this country, so legislators in the South didn't want African Americans to exercise any kind of power. So, they pressured the government to deliberately exclude domestic workers." Gonzalez was referring to the New Deal's exclusion of both domestic and agricultural work from its provisions. Like Gonzalez, many historians have argued that Southern lawmakers insisted on removing both agricultural and domestic labor from many New Deal provisions because these two industries were staffed predominantly by African Americans (Katznelson 2013). Historian Alana Coble (2006, 100) contends that

> Southern legislators feared that a federal program that provided income to blacks would disrupt both the wage and racial structures of the South. Since over three-fifths of Southern African Americans worked either in agriculture or domestic service, the Southern bloc engineered their exclusion from the federally administered Old Age and Survivors Insurance.

Scholars point out that excluding these labor categories to appease racist Southern lawmakers was not the only instance of U.S. federal law harming African Americans and favoring the white supremacist Southern state and local governments during the Jim Crow era (Dixon 2021; Ngai 2004). President Franklin D. Roosevelt, for example, refused to support antilynching legislation that would have protected African Americans from white supremacist terrorism (Perea 2011, 103). The federal government's failure to protect African Americans maintained a plantation-style economy across the South (Dixon 2021).

While Southern lawmakers argued for the exclusion of domestic labor from New Deal laws on racist grounds, Northern lawmakers and administrative staff also raised bureaucratic concerns regarding the inclusion of household labor in social security and unemployment polices. Historian Touré Reed (2020, 176) notes that the "exclusion of agricultural and domestic workers reflected a convergence of political and economic issues." Lawmakers omitted domestic workers from collective bargaining protections using language that reinforced the notion that work done inside the home was something other than labor. State labor laws that expanded the federal legislation explicitly excluded protection for household employment on these same grounds (Palmer 1989, 112).

Mid-Century and the Family Wage

During this time, across industries protected by New Deal labor laws, positive workplace changes reflected workers' organizing efforts in an era of rising industrial unionism (Milkman 1987, 29). This pe-

riod and its associated manufacturing industry is often thought of as
Fordism, referring to Henry Ford, famed auto manufacturer, and to
Detroit's automotive plants. This term is shorthand for a particular
economic arrangement in which workers ceded control over production, guaranteeing stability, in return for relatively decent wages and
hours from industry, while state welfare policy provided a safety net
for unemployment (di Leonardo 2008, 4; Harvey 2003, 187). Historians even dubbed the 1948 pact between auto companies and workers
organizing through labor unions to secure annual wage increases as
the Treaty of Detroit. This treaty set the wage pattern for both union
and nonunion manufacturing sectors, meaning that even those employed in nonunion jobs expected a relatively high wage during the
height of U.S. Fordism.

But as with previous eras, companies and labor unions discrimi-
nated against men of color and women of all races, which prevented
the wholesale incorporation of Fordist and labor union pacts across
the country. Nonetheless, the wages and benefits enjoyed by White
working- and middle-class men transformed the United States
throughout the postwar years into a society with "fairly equally" distributed income (di Leonardo 2008, 4). Wages were high enough in
this era to earn the label *family wage*, which is the term that economists give to the arrangement where only one—typically male—family member has to work outside the home to earn enough to support
the whole family (Fraser 2016, 104). But this conception of a "male
breadwinner" meant that all the reproductive labor typically fell on
the shoulders of female family members who performed housework,
childcare, laundry, and so forth for no wages (Coble 2006, 114).

Meanwhile, in one of the only large-scale disruptions to the gendered division of labor, the demand for factory work during World
War II drew women away from paid domestic service. Nearly two
million women transitioned to industrial labor during and imme-
diately following World War II, as men left positions to enter the
military. According to Coble (2006, 114), "Not only were servants
the largest group of job changers, but domestic service was the only
occupation to lose workers." Historian Ruth Milkman (1987, 103)
chronicled women's dual desire for easier manual labor and a regu-
lated employment industry: one former domestic worker remarked

"I love it here, better than housework. I love machines. In the factory you're finished at the same time every day."

Due to a postwar resurgence of domestic sphere ideology, as men returned to their previous occupations, women struggled to hang on to wartime positions in the face of harassment, ousting, and discrimination. Yet, because postwar production levels topped wartime peaks, employment opportunities still soared for veterans, men of color, and women of all races (Milkman 1987). Despite pressure on women to leave manufacturing labor after the war, their numbers grew and "by the early 1950s, the number of gainfully employed women exceeded the highest wartime level" (Milkman 1987, 100). Accordingly, census data recorded that "personal service: private household," which was the employment category with the largest number of women throughout the nineteenth and twentieth centuries, had dropped to fourth position by 1950 (Coble 2006, 4).

Women's employment in factories, shops, and offices soared following the war, even though innovations in household technology spurred and accommodated the renewal of the domestic goddess image of homemakers. Coble (2006, 119) finds evidence for this in a quote from a popular magazine: "Appliances were the 'new servants,' wrote Mary Roche, the managing editor of *Charm Magazine* in 1955." Similarly, a prominent household economist proclaimed, "The woman who could not afford, or could not find, a servant was not to be pitied—she has simply realized that this was a job which could no longer be delegated to her social inferiors" (Coble 2006, 122). With expanded employment opportunities for women in other fields and time-saving technological advances for household labor, the postwar period saw a decline in domestic work.

Social Movements of the 1960s

The civil rights movement in the mid-1960s, the 1965 Immigration Reform Act, and the second wave of the feminist movement deeply influenced the character and demography of domestic work. Trends toward day work and part-time housekeeping meant that those women still employed in domestic work by the 1950s likely had multiple sources of income or worked simultaneously for many families (Palm-

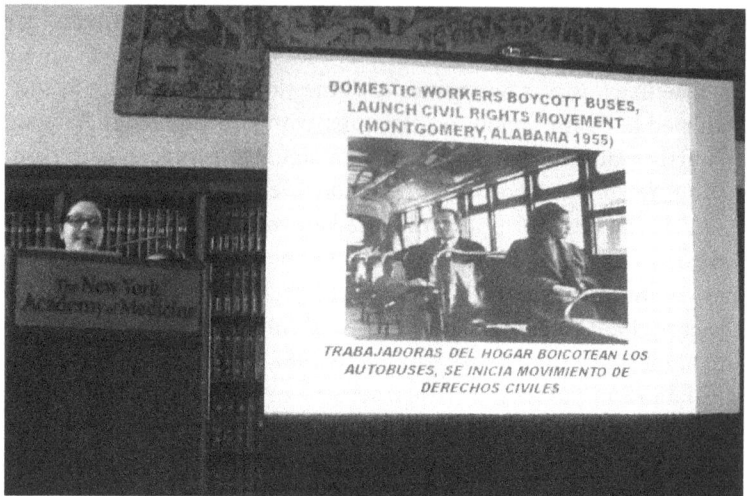

Figure 2.2 Image from slideshow of history of domestic workers' activism during the civil rights movement at DWU convention.

er 1989, xiii). During the 1950s, African American domestic workers formed labor organizations to advocate for themselves and reform the domestic work sector, as historian Premilla Nadasen (2015b) has detailed. The broader civil rights movement, encompassing African American women working in domestic service, also prioritized the expansion of New Deal labor laws to all sectors—including domestic work. The leaders of the 1963 March on Washington highlighted, as one of their ten core demands, "A broadened Fair Labor Standards Act to include all areas of employment which are presently excluded" (Dixon 2021, 10). Yet further amendments to New Deal labor laws, like the Fair Labor Standards Act, continued to exclude domestic and agricultural labor.

It was not until the gains of civil rights organizing and the 1964 passage of the Civil Rights Act that Black American women successfully sought employment beyond household work. Through minimum wage legislation, antidiscrimination laws, and job training programs, Black American women in domestic service could attain stepping-stone career opportunities in other fields (Coble 2006, 149). African American women left domestic employment en masse during this era. Yet, as Nadasen (2015b) demonstrates, these professional moves were largely lateral, toward other reproductive labor positions outside of the home.

During this period, Betty Friedan's *The Feminine Mystique* (1963), a manifesto for second-wave feminists, piqued an "existential crisis" among middle-class homemakers throughout the United States. Newly attuned to the oppressive nature of household labor itself (rather than the profession's degraded status or workers' low status), employers of domestic workers empathized with and saw themselves in solidarity with household workers. In 1960, one young homemaker proclaimed, "It is not work, it's labor, and labor is not valued" (Coble 2006, 131). Writing about the debate within feminist circles, Coble characterizes it as polarized, with "career" women who regarded housekeeping as a drag upon women's liberation on one side and housewives who sought to make household work more valued on the other. "The personal became the political—and as mores changed, women were face to face with political reality in their own homes," Coble writes (131). She concludes that both sides of the debate placed a new value on paid domestic labor, buoying the pay of household employees (130).

At the same time, the 1965 passage of the Immigration Reform Act repealed national exclusionary quotas, lowered the quotas of European nations, and, for the first time, imposed quotas on migration from the Western Hemisphere (Coble 2006, 145). Moreover, this act increased immigration on the basis of occupational status and family unification, and created a five-year naturalization process (146). Combined with the widespread departure of Black American women from domestic work, the opening of immigration in the mid-1960s resulted in a drastic demographic transition within the industry. Caribbean and Latin American immigrants constituted the greatest influx of migrant women into household labor at this time, a pattern that endured beyond the 1960s (157). Afro-Caribbean women, in particular, accounted for one-quarter of household laborers, though they were only one-twentieth of all female employees (158). Ramifications from this period of immigration reform can be seen in the makeup of the domestic work sector, particularly in New York where 78 percent of domestic workers are immigrants to the United States (National Domestic Workers Alliance, n.d.).

1970s–1990s: Neoliberal Globalization

Structural changes in the U.S. economy since the 1970s profoundly affected workers across sectors. Initially, the social movements of the 1960s yielded some benefit in the form of expanded workplace regulations. The 1970 Occupational Safety and Health Act, for example, introduced laws designed to protect workers from hazardous work environments, toxic plants, and deleterious work tasks (Nadasen 2009b). The act, however, applies only to firms with more than fifteen workers, so it generally does not apply to domestic workers who usually work alone in someone's private home. Meanwhile, the Fair Labor Standards Act expanded to include some household laborers in 1974, though legal exemptions again rendered most domestic workers ineligible for overtime and minimum wage laws because the law explicitly excluded "companion services," which includes the labor of babysitters, nannies, personal attendants, and elderly companions (Coble 2006, 4). So, as with previous labor legislation, most domestic workers did not benefit from increasing worker protections.

More pronounced structural changes in the U.S. economy since the 1970s have had a greater effect on workers in the United States and, in fact, around the world. DWU trainings educated workers on this context as well. One evening in 2011, for example, I snuck into the DWU conference room and sat quietly on the floor, having arrived late for a training on care work and the economy. The small room was full. Most people in attendance were DWU members—care workers themselves—from countries across the Caribbean and South and Central America. A few women from West African countries were there, as well as a couple of women from partner organizations representing Filipina and South Asian workers. DWU's staff and board members shuttled in and out of the office door. Volunteers ushered young children to another room to occupy them while their parents attended the event. And latecomers, like me, tiptoed into the room and squeezed themselves into chairs along the back wall and at the large rectangular conference table.

"Let's start with the decline of U.S. manufacturing," the trainer began. At first glance, it may seem odd to begin a class about care work with the collapse of U.S. factory jobs, especially speaking to a room of domestic workers, mostly immigrant women from countries around the world, many of whom have never worked in factories. But the trainer began with manufacturing to historicize the current moment, providing us with an explanation for how and why things have shifted over the past half century. These shifts entailed a transition from a Fordist (discussed earlier) to what we can think of as a *neoliberal* approach to jobs and policy (Harvey 1990, 141).

The DWU trainer explained that the decline of U.S. manufacturing, like so many facets of our lives, "comes back to neoliberal globalization." The terms *neoliberal* and *globalization* are somewhat polysemous, meaning that people use them in various ways to mean slightly different things. But usually, *neoliberal globalization* refers to a set of beliefs about how the world economy should work, including increased economic competition, deregulation (eliminating laws that infringe on how companies and corporations operate), opening domestic markets to foreign companies, and shrinking the role of government. Neoliberal policies eliminate many of the government's functions, including by limiting its ability to spend money on basic necessities such as food, housing, education, transportation, and infrastructure (referred to as *austerity*), or outsourcing some of them to private corporations to deliver in exchange for a profit (referred to as *privatization*) (Ostry, Loungani, and Furceri 2016). A DWU member in attendance frankly summarized these policies, saying that neoliberal globalization means "trying to make more profits off of us." This pithy comment encapsulates many common criticisms of neoliberal globalization and its detrimental effects on working people the world over.

The gains achieved through the Treaty of Detroit for many workers, especially those employed in factories, began to unravel through deliberate policy decisions that facilitated companies' profit accumulation and mobility. Scholars have characterized neoliberal globalization policies as a "confrontation with the rigidities of Fordism," meaning that companies sought to get out of labor pacts in order to realize greater profits, whether by limiting the money companies paid in salaries and benefits or reducing costs spent on ensuring safe workplaces (Harvey 2003, 147). One main route to maximize profits was through outsourcing factories to other parts of the world, or even to regions of the United States with weaker labor laws and lower wages for workers (159). Anthropologist Micaela di Leonardo (2008, 18) argues that neoliberal globalization weakened workers' power to protect themselves and command high wages "through the ever present threat of entire factories decamping elsewhere." She further notes that "labor organizers have labeled the process of labor and communities chasing shifting capital 'the race to the bottom'" or "'reverse Fordism'" (15).

At the same time, politicians and business leaders pushed parallel changes in tax policies and social services, seeking to reduce the amount of taxes that the wealthy and corporations paid into the system, starving necessary services of funding. State and federal governments pursued a path of austerity, eliminating protections for the unemployed and underemployed, the elderly, families with small children, and those with disabilities. Important programs, once administered and funded through the government, were privatized (delivered to consumers for a fee rather than provided to citizens as a right). While the DWU trainer explained these concurrent changes, an audience member remarked, "It's as though government said, 'Not our problem, pay for this out of your own pocketbook,'" crisply summarizing the workings of austerity and privatization.

Due to the loss of high-paying manufacturing jobs and the elimination of social supports to help those who fell on hard times, by the mid-1990s, if not earlier, most families could not afford to subsist on one income. The family wage of the 1950s was no longer offered to most workers. In two-parent homes, that meant that both parents had to seek employment outside of the home. In single-parent homes, it resulted in poverty and even homelessness (Grant et al. 2013). With parents working long hours in relatively poor paying jobs outside the home, a care gap emerged: who could care for children, elderly or infirm adults, or even homes and offices? The DWU trainer explained that, in the United States, caregiving tasks have been commodified or marketized to address this gap, meaning that families (who could afford to) increasingly hired nannies, eldercare providers, and housecleaners to perform caregiving tasks and provide reproductive labor inside the home.

The development of a care gap has entailed these processes of factory outsourcing and globalization, which allowed employers to keep wages unfairly low and rights at a minimum. Globalization—and, in fact, even the construction of factories around the world—also offered a "solution" to the care gap that emerged by encouraging migration to the United States. Having analyzed the causes of migration in myriad places around the world, sociologist Saskia Sassen (1991, 31) argues that "because immigration is thought to result from unfavorable socioeconomic conditions in other countries, it is assumed to be unrelated to U.S. economic needs or broader international conditions." Sassen emphasizes that, despite efforts to structure American immigration via formal policy, migrations follow observable though unintended economic patterns: "The very means commonly thought to deter migration—foreign investment and the promotion of export-oriented growth in developing countries—seem to have precisely the opposite effect" (34). As Caribbean, Asian, and Latin American countries industrialized throughout the late 1960s and 1970s, migration to the United States from those same countries increased.

These migrations, like the low-wage labor sector, have become increasingly feminized over the past thirty years (Sassen 1991, 36), with clear repercussions for domestic workers. Without viable options in their hometowns, the number of women migrating as nurses, nannies, and sex workers has increased (32). Sociologists Barbara Ehrenreich and Arlie Russell Hochschild (2004, 2–3) summarize the situation in this way: "Thanks to the process we loosely call 'globalization,' women are on the move as never before in history. . . . This is the female underside of globalization, whereby millions . . . from poor countries in the South migrate to do the 'women's work' of the North." Building on Glenn's (1992) concept of the *racial division of reproductive labor*, sociologist Rhacel Salazar Parreñas (2005) introduced the concept of the *international division of reproductive labor* to explain the relationship between women's increased migrations and the allocation of reproductive labor around the world.

Reflecting DWU's educational approach, Helen, a DWU board member and longtime nanny, consistently situated her own childcare labor and that of other care workers in terms of these big-picture connections. As she told me, "We contribute so much to this world. I'm not even going to say this nation's economy, to the world's economy." Ai-jen Poo (2011, 52), DWU's founder, notes that, while it is difficult to quantify domestic workers' contributions to the economy because their labor "has not been factored into national labor statistics," "we can estimate these workers' contributions by imagining what would happen if they withheld their labor. If domestic workers went on strike, they could paralyze almost every industry in urban areas." In framing caregiving labor as inextricable from the global economy, Helen marshalled all of these broad economic and political insights, connecting structural economic and immigration issues directly to the social value and importance of domestic work:

> We're either documented or undocumented. We're providing for our families here in the U.S. as well as our families back home, as well as the families we work for. When you think about the load that we as immigrant women—mainly of color—carry, we have the whole world in our hands, literally.

Helen's framing of her own labor and the broader domestic work industry illustrates the interpretation that DWU members often expressed, grounded in DWU trainings like this one on neoliberal globalization. Understanding the value of immigrant women of color's caring labor to "the whole world" was an integral part of DWU's messaging in fighting for passage of the Domestic Workers' Bill of Rights, as we will see in the next chapter.

The Next Twenty Years: The Emerging Care Economy

At the conclusion of the DWU training on neoliberal globalization, a longtime DWU staff member wrote on the dry erase board at the front of the room. "Care economy," she wrote in large red letters. "This means power," she said, before underlining the phrase. The notion of a *care economy* has emerged among researchers and activists over the past couple of decades to characterize the anticipated transition in the United States from an economic system broadly reliant on manufacturing and office work to one where most jobs involve caring for other people.

Why has there been such a boom in the care economy? One reason is that people now live longer than they did a generation ago. Medical anthropologist Maria de la Luz Ibarra (2016, 80) notes that longer life spans "signal a new way of being human, with potentially longer periods of dependency and vulnerability for greater numbers of people." Many will now live for ten, twenty, or thirty years at the end of their

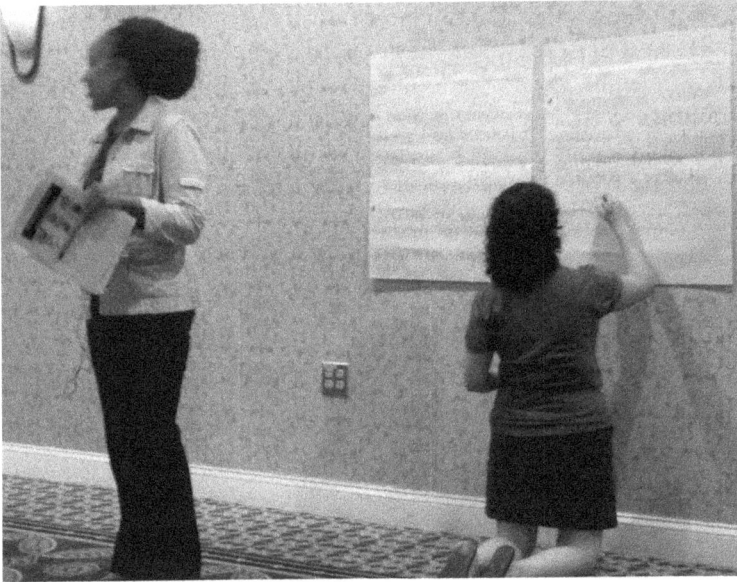

Figure 2.3 DWU board member and director solicit responses during a training on the care economy.

lives reliant on other people to help them dress, eat, walk, and use the bathroom. This prolonged period of dependency may shift what we understand being human to mean. Economists expect that childcare and eldercare jobs will be the largest occupations in the United States by about 2030, and the ranks of home health aides, personal attendants, childcare providers, and elder companions are "expected to grow more than those of any other job in the next decade, according to the Bureau of Labor Statistics" (Donovan and Alarcón 2021, n.p.).

The trainer remarked that organizing all of the people who will likely become care workers in the next decade would "mean real power in this society." Organizing all of the workers who care for children, clean homes, and assist the elderly at the end of their lives into unions and workers' rights group would permit them to exercise their collective political power—to "call the shots in this country," as the trainer powerfully put it, becoming a force for change. That is the long-term goal for care workers: building real power through workers' solidarity with one another that can more fully transform workers' lives and the lives of those for whom they care. In the next chapter, I trace how DWU members and other domestic workers applied these types of trainings to remedy the historic exclusion of their labor sector from U.S. labor law protections by envisioning and passing the New York Domestic Workers' Bill of Rights—the first labor legislation in the country to cover in-home workers.

3

"Tell Dem Slavery Done"

Passing and Implementing the Domestic
Workers' Bill of Rights

One of the first events I attended with DWU members was a small press conference in November 2010 that heralded the implementation of the Domestic Workers' Bill of Rights. DWU held the event in front of Harlem's Harriet Tubman statue. A famed abolitionist, Tubman dedicated her life to liberating enslaved people through the Underground Railroad, risking her own life and freedom in the process. After the Civil War, she worked tirelessly to care for the elderly. Tubman's legacy echoed in the historic significance of DWU's press conference, as a DWU staff organizer proclaimed:

> Several years ago, domestic workers—nannies, housekeepers, and eldercare givers—set out to do something that many thought was impossible. We set out to change labor law. We set out to pull the domestic work industry out of the shadows of slavery and we won.

As we saw in the previous chapter, DWU's political education trainings drew parallels between the experiences of domestic workers throughout U.S. history and those of contemporary care workers, in order to contextualize the practices and norms within New York City's domestic work industry. The selection of Tubman's statue for the historic commemoration of the Domestic Workers' Bill of Rights' passage demonstrates how DWU also linked its publicity and public-facing efforts to the long history of the forced labor and resistance of African-descended women, with the goal of publicizing problems in the sector and inspiring others into action. In particular, DWU's campaign to pass the Domestic Workers' Bill of Rights marshalled the racially oppressive and exploitative history of domestic work in the United States to educate legislators as well as the broader public about the hidden history of reproductive labor.

With the passage of the 2010 Domestic Workers' Bill of Rights, the first law in the United States to extend labor law protections to household workers, New York State set regulations for care worker employers in their private homes—a tricky location for government to enforce laws. The introduction of laws into a new sector involves what social scientists refer to as *the state*, a term that is in some ways synonymous with the term *government*. In this case, *the state* refers to government entities, politicians, and officials who passed and now must enforce the Domestic Workers' Bill of Rights. The U.S. Department of Labor representative that May encountered in Chapter 1 can be thought of as a representative of the state.

In some cases, when the state steps in, it takes an active role. Sociologist Shireen Ally (2009, 88) studied the introduction of labor regulations for household workers in postapartheid South Africa, writing that "the state became a proxy for workers—their articulator, representative, and protector." But, reflecting on the nuances of the care work sector, Ally argues, "It turns out that while the state's efforts assumed paid domestic work is a form of work like any other . . . domestic workers are *not* workers like any other" (95). As we have seen, the bonds that form between caregivers and those they care for and work for make domestic work unique because of the personalism of this type of work. Therefore, implementing the new law in private homes relies on domestic workers' ongoing solidarity with one another, their ability to share insights with one another and to encourage one another to address working conditions directly. DWU offers a formalized space for such solidarity.

In this chapter, I trace the origins and passage of the Domestic Workers' Bill of Rights through activists' recounting of their early legislative activism as well as compromises the group made, showcasing how DWU activism not only reformulated how U.S. labor law applies to domestic work but also how it applies (and doesn't apply) to other employment sectors. I then describe how DWU members and coalition partners worked to inform other domestic workers about the Domestic Workers' Bill of Rights, and how they sought to address limitations of the new law in concert with the New York Department of Labor. This chapter thus illustrates how domestic work advocates commiserated and built solidarity with one another during meetings, and how they strategized about how to address gaps in labor law coverage in order to enforce the new law in a context where no one was conducting door-to-door inspections.

What Would a New Law for Domestic Workers Entail?

Domestic Workers United was founded by Ai-jen Poo, who became president of the National Domestic Workers Alliance in 2007. By 1999, Poo and organizers from the Committee Against Asian American Violence (CAAAV) and Andolan had been fighting to protect the rights of workers "in different Asian communities" for years (Poo 2010, n.p.). Many of their advocacy efforts focused on housekeepers employed in hotels and private homes. When Poo met a Jamaican domestic worker, who described being trafficked and confined by her employers as a teenager, Poo started collaborating with Caribbean, African, and Latina domestic workers to form a labor organization that would uplift domestic work jobs (Ehrenreich 2011).

Using direct-action tactics targeting individual employers, Poo and the early activists she collaborated with initially struggled to get workers' back wages, to liberate them from confinement and trafficking, and to hold employers accountable for abuse and mistreatment (Poo 2010). With two hundred thousand domestic workers employed in private homes in New York City, the fledgling coalition realized that they could not address each individual workplace issue: they had to target the broader system in which negligent or exploitative employers flourished. "As the work evolved, it became clear that grassroots . . . case-by-case fighting wasn't going to give workers the protection they needed," Poo (2011, 46) writes. From these early experiences and insights, Domestic Workers United and the campaign to pass a domestic workers' bill of rights were born.

The small group achieved an early significant victory when it per-suaded the New York City Council to support antitrafficking mea-sures for live-in domestic workers employed through employment agencies. As Helen explained to me, the "first step was to pass leg-islation against the employment agencies in the city" that preyed on undocumented domestic workers like Pamela and Bev, whose stories are told in Chapter 1. In 2003, the newly formed DWU fought for and won a New York City law that required employment agencies to inform workers about minimum standards for job conditions (Poo 2011, 46).

That victory galvanized New York City domestic worker activists, Helen explained: "We couldn't stop there." I met Helen during my first month of participant observation in New York City. She held a leadership position on the DWU board and acted as spokesperson for the group. I often saw her in the office directing staff and volunteers during the day and facilitating meetings and trainings in the eve-nings. She appeared to be in charge of nearly all of the events that I attended. During one protest action early on, while she was complet-ing her headcount of members as they arrived for the demonstration, she joked, "There was a Domestic Workers United before Helen and a Domestic Workers United after," pointing out how seamlessly things ran with her at the helm. As Helen and I established a professional rapport built on our common belief in DWU's organizational mis-sion, I developed immense respect for her skill as a political organizer and her analysis of the U.S. domestic work sector. And, through our conversations, she reconstructed for me the process of envisioning and passing the Domestic Workers' Bill of Rights.

In 2004, DWU planned a gathering for domestic workers called the "Having Your Say Convention." "It was a huge to-do, a huge event," Helen told me. That first convention brought together three hundred New York City housekeepers, nannies, and eldercare pro-viders in a lower Manhattan union hall. The afternoon's emcee wel-comed everyone by saying, "Ladies, we are making history here today. You have a voice, and together we are going places" (Poo 2010, n.p.). The organizers of the convention formed the New York Domestic Worker Justice Coalition, anchored by DWU and partner organiza-tions like Andolan, Adhikaar for Human Rights, Unity Houseclean-ers, Damayan Migrant Workers Association, and Haitian Women for

Haitian Refugees. During the convention, Helen explained, "Workers filled out surveys about what they wanted to see, the changes they would want to see in the industry . . . and through the survey along with the NYU Law Clinic we were able to develop the Bill of Rights." The Domestic Workers' Bill of Rights emerged from nannies, housekeepers, and elder caretakers themselves identifying what they needed to improve and uplift their industry.

Based on the experiences and injustices that they identified (such as disrupted sleep working overnights as eldercare providers, earning less than federal minimum wage for their work, and having no say over the hours that they worked), the Domestic Workers' Bill of Rights' initial provisions offer an important benchmark for dignified jobs across industries. Their survey produced an expansive vision of dignified domestic work jobs and safe, fair treatment of domestic workers. That vision promoted an ideal of work that respected the professionalism and autonomy of domestic workers as well as their entitlement to time off, employment benefits and security, adequate pay, and respect on the job. "We started out with a million and one provisions," Helen joked. She recalled, "Originally, when we started to write the bill, it had two weeks of paid vacation, a $14 per hour rate, health insurance, termination with notice and with severance." The domestic workers and labor leaders who envisioned the Domestic Workers' Bill of Rights hoped it would be a transformative law codifying fair labor standards for the domestic work industry.

However, as we will see, writing legislation entails compromise, so the final version of the Domestic Workers' Bill of Rights was not a perfect reflection of the domestic workers' hopes for their sector. Still, the original provisions envisioned by domestic workers give us a sense of what fairness and dignity for workers could entail. First, the initial version of the law included language stating that domestic workers should receive wages ensuring they could live reasonably comfortably in New York, what economists refer to as a *living wage*. The first version even identified this wage as $14 per hour for domestic workers. The $14 hourly wage did not make it into the final version of the Domestic Workers' Bill of Rights, and its removal reflects a broader trend toward stagnating wages across U.S. industries. The version of the Domestic Workers' Bill of Rights that passed in 2010 simply extended existing minimum wage coverage to this sector. As of 2022, the U.S. federal minimum wage is $7.25 per hour, but this amount has not kept up with the cost of living, meaning it is too low to live on. And it has not kept pace with the productivity gains that corporations have realized either. Had the minimum wage increased at the pace of productivity, it would have been just under $20 per hour in 2017 (Baker 2020).

The average U.S. worker's inflation-adjusted salary has not budged since 1978, despite corporate profits increasing over the same period (Davis and Mishel 2014; Desilver 2018). Wage stagnation results from neoliberal policies enacted over the previous half century, including Congress's refusal to increase the federal minimum wage, interest policies designed to maintain relatively high levels of unemployment, deregulation of finance and other critical industries, and passage of laws that make it more difficult for workers to form unions and to fight for better wages and working conditions (Shermer 2018). In fact, fast-food employees and other service workers have been fighting for a $15 hourly minimum wage since 2010, but as of 2022 they still have not been able to secure this wage.

Early versions of the Domestic Workers' Bill of Rights also included requirements for termination notice and severance pay. Most U.S. workers are *at-will employees*, which means that they can quit and their employer can fire them, at any time for any reason or for no reason at all. In-home domestic workers are especially at risk of abrupt termination, as Danata's frequent terminations demonstrated in Chapter 1. Changes in employers' care work needs can be sudden, due to relocation, death, or children no longer requiring care. In addition, as we saw during COVID-19 when housekeepers, babysitters, and nannies were suddenly unable to go to work for the private families employing them due to a global pandemic, unexpected disruptions to employers' lives may cause them to let domestic workers go or reduce their paid hours. Legislators removed severance pay and termination notice from the Domestic Workers' Bill of Rights' language because they feared it could harm the children and elderly people for whom nannies and home health aides provide care. They worried that requiring a notice of termination and severance pay would pressure employers to retain a substandard domestic employee; this concern reflects the personalism of the domestic industry, discussed at some length in Chapter 1, where caretaking roles represent unique la-

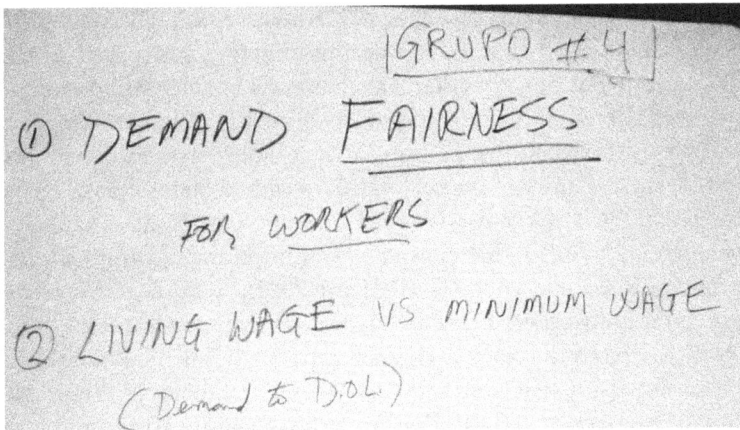

Figure 3.1 Notes written on a large sheet of paper during a discussion about securing living wages for all essential workers.

bor arrangements entailing personal relationships in which the well-being of more than one party (both the worker and those for whom they care) are at issue. This particular tension is unique to care work, although vulnerability to termination is common for U.S. workers who are not protected by a labor union contract.

When domestic workers lose their jobs for any reason, they are left without income. In some industries, when employers fire or lay off a worker, they must pay them a severance, or a portion of their wages. In the United States, severance pay is only typical of jobs with an employment contract, usually negotiated on behalf of workers by their labor union. About 10 percent of workers in the United States are protected by a labor union (Muhl 2001). At-will employees, however, do not have employment contracts and typically do not receive severance pay from their employers (Muhl 2001). Many workers are protected by unemployment insurance: if an employer terminates an employee without a justifiable cause or lays them off due to an economic downturn, most employees in other industries can try to claim unemployment insurance, which their employer paid on their behalf as part of their payroll taxes. Domestic workers, however, very often do not qualify for unemployment insurance, either because they work "off the books" for a private family who does not pay any payroll taxes to the government or because they are classified as independent contractors by home healthcare agencies or house cleaning companies.

Beyond calling for a living wage, termination notice, and severance pay for in-home workers, at that early convention, domestic workers also envisioned including "two weeks of paid vacation" in their law. Many countries around the world legislate paid leave for ten, twenty, or thirty days per year. The United States, however, "is the only OECD [Organisation for Economic Co-operation and Development][1] country that doesn't have minimum paid annual leave implemented at the federal level" (Train 2022). So, while unfortunate for domestic workers like Pearl, whom we met in Chapter 1, who worked around the clock caring for Papa Joe in his final months, it is not surprising that New York State lawmakers removed this provision of two weeks paid vacation from the Domestic Workers' Bill of Rights.

Reducing the Scope of the Domestic Workers' Bill of Rights

The process of reconciling the Domestic Workers' Bill of Rights' original provisions with political expediency was a painful one for domestic worker advocates. Helen recalled:

> It changed a lot and it was painful being a part of that process. For every legislative session we would go back and have to take something out just to appease the legislators and, you know, it was a tough time for many of us. But, we understood that that's what needed to happen for legislators to even pay us attention and to see that we were, one, serious about the work we were doing and, two, that we were serious about changing the industry of domestic workers in this city and in this country.

As Helen suggests, and the early history of domestic labor illustrates, the chance to advocate for the domestic industry was unprecedented and hard won. Thus, domestic worker activists accepted changes to the Domestic Workers' Bill of Rights' protections that would move the law for in-home workers closer to the standard for the majority of U.S. workers, while realizing that very few workers enjoy robust on-the-job protections and benefits in the United States. Unfortunately, the numbers of workers who do have these protections have been dwindling.[2]

Helen and other domestic workers remained upbeat in describing the Domestic Workers' Bill of Rights' final provisions, realizing the magnitude of opposition they faced in introducing legislation. As Helen says, they "lucked out" in passing the law:

> What we were able to luck out with is a forty-hour work week, overtime after forty hours per week, then three days off per year if you're working with the same family. These could be used as personal days, sick days, or vacation days. Then protection from discrimination.

These provisions are "the floor," as she and other DWU members say, for employment protections. These basic employment standards— taken for granted across many industries—like a forty-hour work week, overtime pay, and sick days, did not exist for domestic workers until the 2010 passage of the Domestic Workers' Bill of Rights. "Which," as Helen reminded me, "is amazing because it's the first [law] of its kind in this country's history for domestic workers."

Despite not mandating paid vacation time or a $14 per hour wage for domestic workers, in almost all cases, the final version of the Domestic Workers' Bill of Rights corrects labor law gaps, bringing the domestic work sector in line with other industries. Sexual harassment laws, already on the books for other jobs, now cover New York's in-home workers. The law extended minimum wage coverage and mandated overtime pay after forty hours for domestic workers who live off premises, and after forty-four hours for live-in workers. It also extends workers' compensation insurance to domestic workers.

Moreover, two specific provisions provided domestic workers with standards that exceed existing New York State laws for other employment fields. First, the Domestic Workers' Bill of Rights guarantees one day of rest per week, meaning that by law domestic workers must receive one day off each week (typically unpaid). This clause is especially important for live-in workers. Due to employers' proximity and access, live-in childcare and eldercare providers often work through weekends and overnight without any days off. Second, it stipulates that domestic workers receive "three paid days off after one year of employment." These two aspects of the Domestic Workers' Bill of Rights protect workers who live in the homes of the families for whom they work. As I discuss in Chapter 1, live-in domestic workers often worry that they might be trapped in the homes where they live and work, or be forced to continue working without pay. While some employers may violate these provisions of the Domestic Workers' Bill of Rights, it is the first example in U.S. history of labor regulations designed to protect domestic workers' off-the-clock time and ensure their freedom of mobility.

Finally, the Domestic Workers' Bill of Rights also required the Commissioner of Labor to conduct a feasibility study to examine the possibility of extending collective bargaining rights within the industry. *Collective bargaining* refers to the negotiations that workers and employers enter into in fields where workers are represented by a labor union. It is a right afforded to employees federally through the National Labor Relations Act and, at the state level, through the State Employment Relations Act. You may recall from Chapter 2 that these laws were passed in the 1930s as part of Roosevelt's New Deal and, like other laws passed at that time, these two laws excluded domestic workers from their protections. Because collective bargaining is still expressly outlawed for domestic workers across New York State, the feasibility study offered a step forward (while not fully reversing this historic exclusion). The promise of collective bargaining, of attaining a domestic worker employment "contract," as DWU's then director Priscilla Gonzalez put it, motivated members for the next leg of DWU's campaign.

The Process of Passing a Law

Passing the Domestic Workers' Bill of Rights, even after removal of the more ambitious provisions, still proved a long and arduous process. The New York Domestic Worker Justice Coalition combined street-level protests with frequent lobbying trips to the state capital for nearly ten years. In January 2004, a group of about a dozen DWU members made their first legislative trip to meet with lawmakers in Albany to discuss the need for a Domestic Workers' Bill of Rights. Helen, who said, "I must have been a part of 90 percent of the trips to Albany," explained that DWU "started out doing smaller legislative visits in the early stages of the Bill of Rights campaign." As the organization's membership and power grew, she continued, they recognized the "need to continue to put pressure on the legislators in Albany," which prompted them to organize larger delegations to lobby and protest on behalf of the Domestic Workers' Bill of Rights in Albany. Helen remembers almost two dozen trips over the course of about six years when, as she says, "we trekked to Albany."

The early legislative visits often entailed simply explaining to lawmakers that domestic work is "real" work that should be protected by the same types of laws that protect other job categories. "In meeting after meeting with legislators and their aides, domestic workers were asked questions like, 'What are you talking about? Is this about domestic violence?'" Poo (2011, 54) recalls of those early experiences in Albany. Because many of the lawmakers did not know what domestic labor entailed or dismissed it as nonlabor, women's work, or something other than a profession on which society relies to function, Helen explained that "a lot of the trips to Albany were really about educating the legislators as to what we do as domestic workers in this city; how much we contribute to the city, to the nation, and to the world's economy; and the significance of protection for this workforce." Helen's description of these educational aims captures how DWU sought to teach New York legislators about the value of reproductive labor.

Educating lawmakers consisted of several steps for DWU. First, they had to contend with the notion that care work is illegitimate, that it is somehow not real work. At a large gathering of care workers in lower Manhattan, a childcare worker explained, "They will say it's not real work. I hate when people say that. 'It's not real work. You are just a babysitter.'" Lawmakers are not alone in their misconceptions of domestic work. Given the enduring legacy of the nineteenth-century association of reproductive labor with enslaved women, servants, and housewives, legislators—like many Americans—still regarded domestic work as "something other than work" (Hondagneu-Sotelo 2001). Helen savvily and insistently refuted this characterization throughout our many conversations. In one instance, she re-enacted the message that DWU members delivered to legislators, proclaiming, "These workers are real workers with real families, real lives, and this is a real industry that needs to be protected, it needs to be uplifted, and it needs to be treated with respect and dignity." To make their arguments more powerful, DWU members often emphasized that "domestic work is real work" in advocating for extending labor laws to this sector. In this process, they educated legislators, employers, and other activists about the history and importance of care work to both U.S. and international economies. Meetings with legislators and public demonstrations were, as Helen said, a "pathway into pushing for this work to be recognized and for the industry to be recognized, and also a lot of it was just really educating the legislators because this work is so important and it's such a hidden work and such an invisible work."

Carrying signs with their slogan, "Respect the work that makes all other work possible" and donning their "Tell Dem Slavery Done" T-shirts, DWU members and allies embarked on an educational campaign that drew on history, social analysis, and personal sentiment about care work and its distribution. DWU's slogan "Tell Dem Slavery Done" reflects the legal codification of domestic workers as falling outside of U.S. labor law, and it resonated with and pressured legislators to take action on behalf of a historically exploited group of workers. Educating lawmakers also called attention to links between domestic labor conditions and historical injustices of slavery, and it permitted DWU activists to directly address the racist roots of their industry's exclusion from labor law. Like the Tubman statue in front of which DWU members chose to announce the passage of the Domestic Workers' Bill of Rights, their legislative visits and broader publicity efforts drew these historical associations between the enslavement of African women and ongoing exclusion of immigrant domestic workers from most labor protections prior to the passage of the Domestic Workers' Bill of Rights.

DWU's framing of the Domestic Workers' Bill of Rights as a corrective for the historical atrocities of slavery, segregation, and institutionalized racism was especially effective in persuading lawmakers. For example, urging then Governor Cuomo to sign the Domestic Workers' Bill of Rights once it passed the Senate, Gonzalez wrote, "Domestic workers have suffered in the shadows of slavery for generations." And again, later, at the Domestic Workers' Bill of Rights' 2010 signing, then Governor David Patterson referenced the race-based exclusion of domestic workers from labor protections, proclaiming, "Today we correct a historic injustice by granting those who care for the elderly, raise our children, and clean our homes the same essential rights to which all workers should be entitled" (Matthews 2010). The passage of the Domestic Workers' Bill of Rights reversed, at least for New York State, centuries of legally codified informality, exploitation, and coercion in the industry. And, in framing the Domestic Workers' Bill of Rights as a remedy for historical racism and its ongoing effects in the lives of working women of color, DWU members claimed the legislation as both a labor victory and a civil rights initiative.

Regulating Domestic Work?

With the introduction of labor law in this sector, the Domestic Workers' Bill of Rights established regulations for domestic work. Typically, *regulation* refers to laws that a government passes to ensure intentional and specific oversight or intervention in business activity or commerce. Often, regulations arise in response to specific problems. For example, Ralph Nader famously campaigned for automobile regulations in the 1970s, following hundreds of auto accident deaths. These regulations compelled auto manufactures to standardize seat belts and other safety features on cars and trucks they sold in the United States. Other examples, from child labor laws to anti-trust regulations, illustrate how regulation can shape an industry.

Overtime rules, sexual harassment laws, and minimum wage laws are all also regulations. But, as we have seen, until the 2010 New York State Domestic Workers' Bill of Rights none of those regulations covered domestic workers. Similar legal omissions for domestic work exist in country after country, including the United Kingdom, Taiwan, Hong Kong, Canada, Turkey, and many Middle Eastern countries (Anderson 2000; Chin 1998; Constable 1997). Labor laws and government regulations often exclude domestic employment, frequently by name as was the case in the United States, relegating reproductive labor to antiquated assumptions of unremunerated "women's work" or to "informal" and "survival job" niches (Duffy 2011). In places where laws do exist, they often dovetail with immigration statutes. Sometimes regulations curtail worker independence and mobility via stratified visa categories. In other cases, immigration policies force workers further into legal liminality as undocumented or guest workers (Glenn 2012; Lan 2006). These types of laws tend to regulate or police workers themselves rather than ensure the safety and fairness of their jobs. In recent years, more and more countries (and territories inside countries) have adopted laws such as the Domestic Workers' Bill of Rights that aim to regulate the work conditions rather than the workers. The precedent-setting Domestic Workers' Bill of Rights—and how DWU members supported its implementation—offers useful insights for these similar initiatives as well as for workers in other sectors fighting for basic labor protections.

Solidarity Required to Make the Law Meaningful

In the months following the 2010 Domestic Workers' Bill of Rights victory, DWU members and their allies—who I discuss in the next chapter—began to address some of the limitations of the new law as well as the difficulty of implementing it in private homes. While the Domestic Workers' Bill of Rights has extended minimum protections to this sector, many questions remain regarding how to enforce the new laws. For example, the law provides workers and employers who are familiar with its stipulations a basis for negotiating a fair contract. But, like most American labor laws, it is fundamentally reactive. The laws become important once they have been violated; by and large, workers and employers are unaware of or unwilling to adopt these practices proactively. And, as we would expect, the U.S. Department of Labor does not conduct door-to-door inspections in people's private residences. The peculiarities of the industry that have historically made domestic workers vulnerable—the gendered and racial division of labor that naturalizes caregiving as nonlabor; dispersed, isolated work sites; the legal liminality that many migrant women report; and endemic racism and sexism—also are untouched by the new law. Finally, the Domestic Workers' Bill of Rights' stipulations omit part-time and occasional care workers.

Relatively few domestic workers outside of DWU were aware that the Domestic Workers' Bill of Rights codified domestic workers as deserving of basic rights and protections under New York State law. With support of the New York Department of Labor, DWU, and the Domestic Worker Justice Coalition, the same groups that gathered at earlier domestic worker conventions to write and pass the Domestic Workers' Bill of Rights embarked on a Know Your Rights campaign in late 2010, championing the new legislation under the banner "A New Day, A New Standard." The campaign included a hotline for domestic workers to call for information, a website, and a booklet that explained in detail how the new law might affect workers and their employers. Most of the outreach entailed activist domestic workers once again hitting the streets, parks, libraries, playgrounds, and on-line discussion boards to educate care workers about the Domestic Workers' Bill of Rights and encourage them to attend DWU meetings. At campaign meetings, DWU members brainstormed about how to spread the word to both domestic workers and those who employ them.

During my participant observation, I frequently attended meetings at the DWU office. It seemed as though the space hosted a different group of members and activists each evening of the week. In fall 2012, I attended a campaign meeting where DWU members debated how to best ensure that passage of the Domestic Workers' Bill of Rights would actually improve the lives of domestic workers. The group acknowledged that many domestic workers' desperation drives them to accept jobs that fall well below the standards for dignity and respect that DWU members fight for. A single, unmarried DWU member without children remarked:

> A lot of domestic workers who take those [poorly paid, exploitative] jobs have priorities and families. They are struggling out there. Some are really struggling. If I had kids to feed, I would have [fed them] by any means necessary. I am going to take care of someone's children, and in the meantime, my child is going to suffer. I have to accept this because I can't afford to be homeless. I can't afford to not feed my kids.

Then another member opined, "The bill is a step in the right direction for people with no days off and no vacation pay." As DWU members discussed the impact of the Domestic Workers' Bill of Rights on vulnerable domestic workers, they highlighted how the law's passage might not be enough to protect domestic workers. The conversation came around to two questions: How to empower other care workers to advocate for themselves, especially if they were undocumented immigrants? And, how to ensure fair wages and working conditions for those without one stable employer?

Ensuring that the Domestic Workers' Bill of Rights protects workers and improves working conditions requires changing perceptions about the work and about the role of immigrant laborers in the United States. For example, replying to the above comment that the bill was "a step in the right direction," Deb, a longtime DWU activist and board member who worked full time as a home healthcare provider, responded to the group, arguing, "You have to eliminate that fear that people are superior to us." Another member spoke up, "Deb, it comes from, when we come here, your family and friends are telling you things about immigration. They are fearful of everything."

As the exchange above illustrates, many activists worry that undocumented domestic workers or those with family obligations will not pursue wage theft or other claims out of fear of job loss or retaliatory detainment or deportation. At another meeting following the passage of the Domestic Workers' Bill of Rights, a domestic worker and activist reflected on the effort she dedicated to letting others know about the new law. Through her outreach, she learned of the denigrating working conditions that many domestic workers faced regardless of their citizenship status, ethnicity, or nationality. These stories, she said, "empowered her to realize that even if you are documented, you are treated the same. It has nothing to do with immigration status but with the unprotected industry harkening back to slavery."

Another DWU member pointed out that the provisions of the Domestic Workers' Bill of Rights only pertain to full-time workers, not part-time domestic workers or intermittent workers. In response, Deb noted that both part-time and occasional domestic workers often "combine three and four jobs in a day" to cobble together a base salary that could support their basic needs. Pamela, whose critique of the precarity associated with agency work I described in Chapter 1, argued, "This is not the exception. Every morning they take them from the cold," referencing the hiring practice in some Brooklyn neighborhoods, where employers pick up day-laboring nannies, housekeepers, and eldercare providers who congregate in front of agencies. The employers pay them for the day's work at a dismal rate without any ongoing responsibilities to that employee. "We have to protect these women," she declared.

Agreeing, another member added, "Many families cannot afford childcare, so they share the cost with a second family, but why should that nanny not benefit under the Bill of Rights?" These conversations drew attention to the limits of the Domestic Workers' Bill of Rights in protecting part-time care workers (those who work less than a forty-hour week for one employer) or those who work for multiple families in a week. Nanny-shares have become a very common arrangement, allowing employers to save money by hiring a childcare provider for one or two days per week. A friend or neighbor will then hire the same nanny to work on the other days. This set-up provides employers with flexibility but, as the DWU member pointed out, it prevents caregivers from claiming benefits that only accrue after working forty hours for the same family. In the case of home healthcare, it is very common for elder companions or home health aides to care for one patient during the weekdays and then supplement their wages by providing live-in care for another patient on Saturdays and Sundays.

Campaign meetings provided opportunities for members to express solidarity with one another, to consider the law's limitations, and to suggest improvements through their Department of Labor partnership. Department of Labor representatives did not attend these meetings but met with a smaller cohort of advocates to assess the best way to expand these protections. A November 2010 Department of Labor report on the feasibility of New York domestic workers forming a labor union noted:

> Most domestic employers only have one domestic employee. However, some domestic workers are employed by multiple families part time each week—and some may work only a partial day for a given employer every two or four weeks. This complicates the question of what an appropriate bargaining unit for domestic workers would be. (18)

These detailed insights into the complications of applying the Domestic Workers' Bill of Rights and extending bargaining protections to this workforce came from Department of Labor collaborations with DWU and its members' input.

Building Solidarity amid the Introduction of Labor Law

These brief exchanges during campaign meetings as well as their influence on the Department of Labor's report demonstrate why many domestic work activists view the Domestic Workers' Bill of Rights as a crucial but insufficient first step toward meaningful transformation in the care work sector. These remarks above as well as others I heard during meetings illustrate the central role of solidarity in how domestic work activists strive to advocate for themselves and one another following the Domestic Workers' Bill of Rights' passage.

Domestic Workers United members deployed many strategies, including commiserating and building solidarity with one another during meetings. In meetings and in conversations, DWU members consistently tacked between their own personal experiences and evaluations of domestic work and their broader awareness of the hardships, exploitation, and fear other women endure due to their immigration status or familial responsibilities. Deb acknowledged, for example, that "people are beginning to feel a little more respected. There is still some abuse. There's still a lot of domestic workers who are afraid to talk about it. There's still so much work to make this bill really work for both employers and employees of domestic work." Helen explained to me her vision of the implementation of the Domestic Workers' Bill of Rights this way:

> I'm only one in the millions that exist. I want for other workers to feel the same way, to feel that level of pride and that level of recognition and that level of "Wow, I don't have to fight this on my own. There's so many more of us fighting this," or, better yet, "The fight has already been fought, and the regulations are in place, the law is in place, and employers know how to make it work so the job is done."

Helen's compelling vision is the motivation that keeps DWU members coming back to meetings, attending protests, and trekking across the state and across the country to protest for domestic worker rights.

In the early part of 2011, at monthly campaign meetings, DWU members strategized about the best ways to spread the word about the Domestic Workers' Bill of Rights and bring more members to the

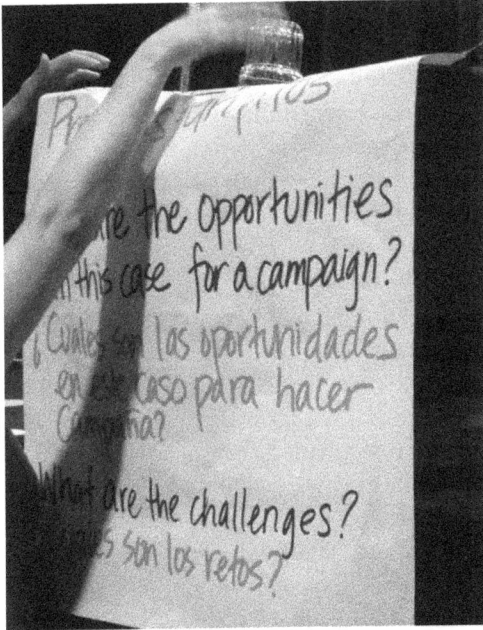

Figure 3.2
Discussion prompts written on a large sheet of paper during a strategy session for the campaign to educate NYC domestic workers and employers about the passage of the Domestic Workers' Bill of Rights.

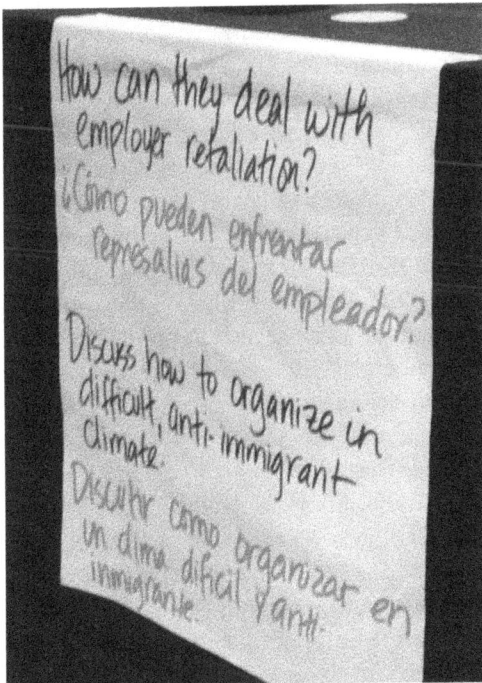

Figure 3.3
Notes written on a large sheet of paper that identify some barriers to successfully recruiting additional members to Domestic Workers United and allied organizations.

organization. At one meeting, members set a goal for how many new members they planned to recruit by the following month. Because domestic workers remain dispersed and isolated in their employers' private homes, ensuring that the provisions in the Domestic Workers' Bill of Rights have an impact on the industry requires recruiting domestic workers unfamiliar with DWU to meetings and introducing them to DWU's vision. "We have to commit to [each] bringing one or two people to next month's meeting," the DWU director said, "so we have a sense of how much womanpower it will take for us to organize two hundred thousand domestic workers," which is the estimated number of New York City's nannies, housekeepers, and eldercare providers. Pamela did not set a goal, lamenting that "at first it's hard to get people to come because they are afraid. They don't know if the place is the right place to be." Meva, a nanny and newer DWU member introduced in Chapter 1, agreed, saying, "I'll try to bring people here, but it is so frustrating, I don't know what to say. . . . Can I take them by the hair and say, 'Stop complaining and come to the center?'" Another member noted that while she was late to that evening's meeting, "Come tomorrow, out in the field, I'll be trying to see what I can do. Got two members, so I will be out there working, doing my part."

Referring to her own circumstances as an undocumented immigrant as well as the circumstances of many of her family members and friends, Pamela added, "Some of us are not U.S. citizens that can go out there and do what we want to do," expressing the fear that prevents some undocumented domestic workers from organizing. "This is why we *organize*," Deb emphatically replied. "The weak can help the strong, go hand-in-hand with each other. And that's organizing. Put our heads together and think what will help us all." When Deb said, "that's organizing," she referred to a political process of educating community members to join together and advocate for themselves, which she also understands as an expression of and a platform for solidarity. "We can move forward if we stick together," she said. Summing up the situation, another woman added, "Some of us, what we get is kind of livable. Some don't get any at all. We've got to fight." This exchange highlights some of the tensions and barriers that DWU members encounter trying to recruit other domestic workers and to educate them about improving the domestic work sector. For some workers, their immigration status, financial desperation, or social networks may discourage them from participating in labor activism. In other cases, domestic workers' wide range of working conditions, salaries, and benefits (varying from "livable" to "nothing at all") can impose barriers to solidarity. In addition, care workers' sense of connection or obligation may discourage them from speaking up about the new wage protections, especially if they have developed close emotional bonds with their charges.

Similarly, at another campaign meeting, members discussed the challenge of organizing in psychologically sensitive terms. Pamela explained it this way:

> As women, a lot of times we suppress our feelings, we push aside our feelings. Going out there, reaching out to people, we feel rejected. When we reach other people, we reach ourselves. We have expectations for other people, but when they disappoint us, it's not necessary to reach back to your expectation of them. But don't stop reaching out. A lot of us have fears. We don't love ourselves. But don't stop.

Pamela's reflection on the process of recruiting and reaching new members encapsulates how DWU provides not only training, political education, and practical organizing but also a solidarity space for domestic workers. Helen described this aspect of DWU meetings:

> Because of the work I do as a nanny, I knew there was always a space for us. . . . I thought that there should always be a space for us as workers to really talk or have shared space where we could share our experiences, our working situations, or whatever.

The process of fighting for the implementation of the Domestic Workers' Bill of Rights in private homes illuminates DWU members' sense of solidarity and shared struggle. In this sense, DWU meetings and outreach efforts reflect Christina Sharpe's (2018, 130) definition of care as "shared risk." Supporting another member who earlier spoke about a trying work situation, a DWU member prefaced her question to the group by saying, "I have to tell Ann to hold strong or else you will just wither away." This sentiment was common in the meetings and conversations that I observed. Meva explained, "It's not just about rights. It's about community building, empowering us to feel secure to go to the job and ask for your rights, knowing that somebody's going to take care of you."

Emboldening Domestic Workers

Familiarity with the Domestic Workers' Bill of Rights could change workers' perspective on their labor or embolden them to leverage it during interviews and negotiations. Helen had recently negotiated a contract stipulating her salary, schedule, overtime, and vacation for a position caring for two children whom she described as "bags of fun and bags of work." She attributed her ability to negotiate the benefits of her recent position to the bill's passage and explained it this way:

> I let employers know from the interview, "There's this bill that's been passed and I've been active in seeing that this bill got passed and here's what the bill is, and this is exactly what I'm looking for." For me, I took what in the bill worked for me—which was a forty-hour work week, because never before in doing this work in over twenty years had I worked a forty-hour work week. Never before had I had a written contract, so that was something extra that I was also able to bargain for after the passage of the bill. Even though a contract is not in the bill, it became . . . an added tool for me to have in securing the job that I'm currently on.

Evelyn, a longtime DWU member and full-time nanny, also told me that the bill's passage bolstered her ability to negotiate with employers. Entering the job search with years of DWU membership and experience behind her, Evelyn felt she was able to negotiate salary, schedule, and autonomy for herself. At the time we spoke, she had recently found a new childcare position and told me this:

> I really hope that this works out between us. She's been paying my taxes, doing all she's supposed to do as an employer. She knows everything that she needs to know about Domestic Workers United. From day one, I walked into her house, I told

her who I am, and I also told her I'm a member of Domestic Workers United. I am actually on the board of directors and I have a great passion for the work that domestic workers do. I want her to know all about it, because there are times I need her to work with me. If I switch days with her—I have congress coming up in May, we've already spoken about it, I want to leave Friday for D.C., we've already switched the days. This is the kind of working relationship, people who respect you and who you can respect. I have the most utmost respect for them because they do respect me. This is something that can really have a nice, positive feel to it.

Evelyn's employment arrangement encapsulates the "dignity and respect" principles for which DWU members fight: Evelyn felt comfortable introducing herself both as a care worker and as an activist, bringing her full self to her role, she negotiated with her employer for flexibility in her work schedule, and she described her employer as doing "everything she needs to do," including paying Evelyn "on the books" (by deducting payroll taxes for Evelyn and paying employer taxes). Evelyn found both the formality of this role and its open communication and flexibility as indicative of the mutual respect that she and her employer have for one another. She also identified tangible benefits from the passage of the Domestic Workers' Bill of Rights, noting that:

It makes life easier because they understand that this is a real job, and I need to treat my domestic worker as a human being, and so it's helping. It's a slow process, but it's helping, it's really helping. I think people are understanding why taking care of somebody else's kid is not easy. So, [they think to themselves] "I really need to have that dialogue and have that open communication with the domestic worker."

Since the passage of the Domestic Workers' Bill of Rights in New York, six other states have passed similar legislation. In 2011, the International Labor Organization of the United Nations passed The Convention on the Rights of Domestic Workers, illustrating the potential power of this workforce. Passing legislation is a critical first step in protecting care workers. Yet, as the trainer in the previous chapter intimated, the laws themselves do not equate to "real power"—yet. The next chapter describes how DWU members engaged in coalition building to strengthen their influence. Recalling this effort, Poo (2010, n.p.) writes, "It became clear that we would not only need to continue building our base of domestic workers, but that we would also need to significantly expand our base of support among other social sectors" by recruiting allies from other industries and interest groups.

4

"No Unlikely Allies"

Building Power through Solidarity
across Communities

At a national meeting of domestic worker organizations in 2011, Ruth, a longtime organizer and former nanny, reflected on the Domestic Workers' Bill of Rights' passage and on the pivotal importance of deep alliances:

> In 2010, we passed the nation's first Domestic Workers' Bill of Rights. After more than seven decades of exclusion, we broke open the path to bringing U.S. labor law into the twentieth century, and we didn't do it alone. Throughout the six-year campaign, we reached out to as many individuals, groups, and organizations as possible—many of you here today. We quickly learned that, in the struggle for dignity and respect, there is no such thing as an unlikely ally. From unions and women's organizations to congregations, immigrant rights and student groups, everyone had a story to share and a deep connection to the rallying cry of our movement: "We have a dream that one day all work will be equal."

As Ruth emphasizes, the Domestic Workers' Bill of Rights campaign drew in supporters from across New York—no group or individual would be an improbable partner in their fight. DWU's campaign to protect domestic workers garnered support from a cross-section of workers, students, and activists in other arenas. "Everyone has a connection to this work," Ruth explained to me one afternoon in the DWU office, recalling the individual trade unionists, politicians, and activists she met who shared stories of their mothers and grandmothers who had worked as washerwomen and housekeepers. Others told her of experiences of being cared for by a nanny in their youth or watching their own parent leave home before sunrise to clean and care in another family's house before returning home well after dark. And still other people Ruth spoke to fondly appreciated the caregivers who allowed them or their parents to live out their lives in their own homes by providing around-the-clock care and support during their later years. DWU's approach to building alliances drew on these personal bonds forged through experiences with caring; in this case, the personalism of care work meant that DWU's activism resonated with everyone who had these close connections.

In this chapter, I describe how DWU enacted a community organizing approach, sometimes referred to as *community unionism*, by joining together with a diverse group of allies. I focus on the role played by DWU's coalition partner Jews for Racial and Economic Justice, a group that had supported DWU's efforts to pass the Domestic Workers' Bill of Rights by organizing employers of domestic workers to stand with domestic workers in the fight to improve employment conditions in private homes. The coalition was critical, first, in passing the Domestic Workers' Bill of Rights and, later, in educating employers about their responsibilities under the Domestic Workers' Bill of Rights and modeling new forms of negotiation and cooperation between employers and domestic workers. This chapter describes the variety of strategies and tactics through which DWU's collaborations built a shared sense of commitment to domestic worker justice, drawing on the personalism of the industry to establish bonds with domestic work employers and workers in other sectors. I conclude by describing one especially powerful event at which workers across industries and those who rely on the labor of care workers used narrative and emotional appeals to build a collective sense of solidarity.

Building Power through Community Unionism

DWU's broad coalition reflects the inventiveness of community unionism, an approach to improving labor conditions in industries when workers cannot gather together on the factory floor, for fear that the company employing them will retaliate by moving to another state or even to another country. In other instances, undocumented workers worry that if they advocate for themselves in their worksites, they will risk deportation or detention. In such situations, they employ other strategies to improve their working conditions, like recruiting religious leaders to advocate on their behalf or strategically targeting company stakeholders for public accountability campaigns. Part of the reason community unionism is so powerful is that it marshals wider circles of influence, such as religious, cultural, ethnic, and transnational groups, allowing workers to join with communities to advocate for shared goals and to employ broader tactics than typical shop-floor labor organizing (Nadasen 2009b).

Because care workers' workplaces are dispersed, in private homes, a community unionism approach was necessary. DWU members used community unionism in lobbying for the passage of the Domestic Workers' Bill of Rights and, later, in outreach campaigns to inform others that the law had passed and to explain how home-based labor could be valued like other work. Poo (2010) relays that, after DWU's initial lobbying trip to Albany, the group realized that they had to build power beyond domestic workers to convince lawmakers to support the bill's passage. DWU began reaching out to universities, synagogues, churches, and labor unions and educating their members about domestic workers' issues. "By opening that kind of space to all the people who were interested in our struggle, we developed a core group of supporters who could lead independent organizing in their own networks," Poo (2010, n.p.) writes. Support for DWU flourished as their allies took it on themselves to educate and build support in their own communities. Legislators might have been able to ignore busloads of domestic workers arriving in Albany week after week and month after month. But DWU's support cut across demographics, including other workers across New York City, employers of domestic workers, and religious groups. Legislators simply could not ignore the coalition that DWU and their allies built.

For DWU, building power for the domestic work sector also entailed "building worker-to-worker solidarity" through reciprocal support for workers in other arenas (Poo 2010, n.p.). A labor union called BJ 32 represents building staff and janitorial workers, including those who work as doormen in Manhattan's high-rise apartment buildings. They joined Domestic Workers United's campaign early on, as their shared workplaces drew BJ 32 members into contact with care workers entering and exiting employers' apartments. Poo (2010, n.p.) explains that "doormen hear the workers' stories of abuse, they are the ones who help workers into cabs after late nights of babysitting, and they are also the shoulders to cry on when someone is fired without notice or severance pay." BJ 32 hosted DWU's tenth anniversary gala (described in the Introduction) in their union hall, where the union's president, who also served as the chair of DWU's anniversary gala, declared, "The domestic worker's movement stands as a beacon of hope. . . . They are the future of the labor movement," gesturing toward the revitalizing role that this multiracial coalition of women workers and their allies played in fighting for the working class. DWU's successful advocacy for the Domestic Workers' Bill of Rights demonstrated the power that workers can wield when they join together.

Domestic workers also found natural allies among agricultural workers, also historically excluded from U.S. labor laws like the Fair Labor Standards Act. Along with groups like Jobs with Justice, DWU and the New York Justice for Farm Workers campaign organized a forty-hour fast to highlight the farm industry's injustices (Poo 2010). During my fieldwork, I joined DWU members at a variety of collective actions, including May Day rallies, rallies in solidarity with tomato growers (at the Union Square Trader Joe's grocery store), and large union rallies across the East Coast. Given DWU's deep and broad alliances, their vision of "dignity and respect" encompasses broader critiques of neoliberal economic policy and American income inequality as well. In the wake of the 2008 economic crisis and during the ensuing recession, DWU members were out in front of large protests calling for finance reform, debt forgiveness, and federal minimum wage increases. DWU members and I frequently attended marches and held teach-ins at Zuccotti Park, and DWU invited Oc-

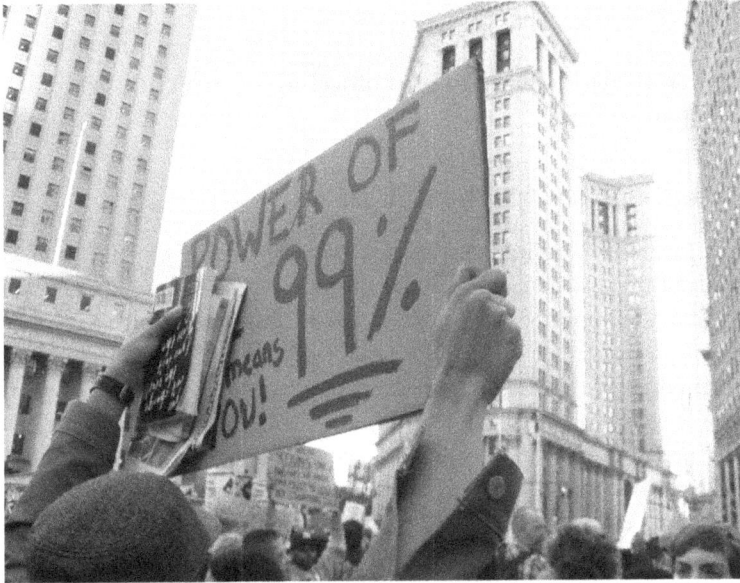

Figure 4.1 Image of a handwritten sign from a large march during the Occupy Wall Street protests that reads, "The power of the 99% means you."

Figure 4.2 Image of a sign from a large march during the Occupy Wall Street protests that reads, "Workers' Rights Are Human Rights."

cupy Wall Street leaders to their offices to conduct trainings on the economic collapse.

Shalom Bayit and Employers for Justice

I attribute my own introduction to DWU to its ability to build sound and enduring alliances. In 2004, I moved to New York City and accepted a temporary position as an event coordinator with the organization Jews for Racial and Economic Justice (JFREJ). JFREJ had formed in the 1990s, as stated on their website, with the goal of "building a more just society, [and] to offer a place where Jewish identity and commitment to social justice are not at odds" (JFREJ, n.d.), actively building alliances across the city in campaigns for racial, immigrant, and economic justice. While I was working for JFREJ, the organization was collaborating with DWU on passing city and state labor laws to protect domestic workers. My work at the time, helping to plan the organization's annual fundraising event, didn't bring me into direct contact with the group's activism. It wasn't until years later, after the 2010 passage of the New York Domestic Workers' Bill of Rights, that I reconnected with JFREJ activists involved in fighting for its passage. Just as I'd done with DWU, I contacted JFREJ and offered to volunteer, citing my previous experience helping to organize their fundraising efforts. That year, the annual fundraiser and celebration—the Rabbi Marshall T. Meyer Risk Taker Awards—was commemorating the passage of the New York Domestic Workers' Bill of Rights and I was eager to contribute.

To support DWU's fight for a Domestic Workers' Bill of Rights, JFREJ began a Shalom Bayit (Peace in the Home) campaign, aiming to recruit and educate people who hire nannies, eldercare providers, and housekeepers, and to organize these employers to take action to improve domestic work. This effort produced the Employers for Justice network. As part of their effort to support DWU's fight for a Domestic Workers' Bill of Rights, and like JFREJ, the broader organization it is a part of, the Shalom Bayit campaign joined politics with religious community. Employers reached out to one another at synagogues, seder events, and through parenting networks. They encouraged rabbis to give sermons on issues affecting domestic workers and on how families employing domestic workers could make minor yet critical improvements in their day-to-day practices. DWU's strategy of joining with employers was novel because most efforts to improve workers' lives and working conditions adopt an adversarial approach to employers; indeed, as we will see in the next chapter, DWU also engages in direct action against individual employers. But domestic work is unique, given the highly personal nature of the labor. Bringing employers with workers together, as allies, to improve workplace practices is therefore a meaningful avenue to change.

Many of the events organized by the Shalom Bayit campaign used cultural traditions and holidays as opportunities to educate and inform others about the Domestic Workers' Bill of Rights campaign. For example, in 2008, the Shalom Bayit campaign celebrated a Passover seder at a public park in Lower Manhattan. They invited DWU members to join and to give presentations about the Domestic Workers' Bill of Rights during the event. One DWU member who presented at the event later recalled her experiences on DWU's website, writing:

> I explained that while we accept appreciation from our employers by words, what we really needed was appreciation by action. I further stressed that domestic work is a priceless job and a valuable service that we provide to our employers. Our employers cannot put a cost on loving and caring for their families. As domestic workers, we give a lot and receive very little. I challenged employers to . . . support the Domestic Workers' Bill of Rights. After my speech, three employers [of domestic workers] at the seder said they will support our Domestic Workers' Bill of Rights.

This domestic worker's recollection offers a sense of how, through DWU's partnership with the Shalom Bayit campaign, employers of domestic workers might see their role hiring a housecleaner or home healthcare provider as a political act with ramifications, newly understanding themselves as political actors by supporting domestic workers. Without the analysis and activism offered through their collaboration with DWU, employers of domestic workers might not see their role as an opportunity to enact fair labor principles—this is especially so because, as we will see, domestic work employers often do not even consider themselves employers in the same way that they might think of a company CEO or store manager.

DWU members also recalled expanding their social networks and developing meaningful friendships through the collaboration with JFREJ. When Jean and I discussed the long process of lobbying to pass the Domestic Workers' Bill of Rights, she proudly recalled her early trips to Albany as emblematic of her admiration for the partnership DWU and JFREJ had established. Jean described walking the legislative hallways in Albany with a rabbi whom she regarded as a mentor. Jean told me that, both born in July, she and the rabbi had a lot in common and shared many interests. She said that the rabbi told her, "'I'm here to support you.' She gave me great ideas. She really boosted my confidence about talking with legislators." Jean's recollection illustrates just one facet of the organizational and personal partnerships forged through the coalition: by working and strategizing with experienced allies, newer activists gained confidence, which in turn, built momentum behind DWU's agenda.

Collaborations between the two organizations didn't simply take place in the state house or at services. At annual fundraising events, like the 2010 Rabbi Marshall T. Meyer Risk Taker Awards, JFREJ and DWU members came together to celebrate both their alliance and the passage of the Domestic Workers' Bill of Rights. The audience was filled with DWU members, JFREJ members, and activists from other organizations across New York City. Members of the Shalom Bayit campaign had made kippot (also known as yarmulkes, or skullcaps) by hand, and gave them out as tokens of gratitude for the DWU members and the employers of domestic workers who had traveled to Albany to lobby beside DWU members. The gesture was intended to recognize the critical contribution of employers of domestic workers acting in solidarity with care workers, which helped ensure the success of the Domestic Workers' Bill of Rights campaign. Inviting these activist employers to the podium, one young activist explained:

> We made these yarmulkes because those who take the bold step to identify themselves as employers [of domestic workers] are doing a Jewish, praiseworthy, and righteous thing. We are

honored to be able to present these yarmulkes as a token of the deep and crucial work that employers have done to bring us to this moment.

After these words, employers and DWU members in the audience donned the colorful, handpainted kippot depicting peace doves and rainbows. Then, two of the activist employers who had led the charge to support DWU stood at the podium and, in turn, invited those of us in the audience to stand:

Stand up if you are a member of Domestic Workers United!

Stand up if you are a domestic worker!

Stand up if you are an employer of a domestic worker and you believe in justice for domestic workers!

Stand up if you were JFREJ staff!

Stand up if you were ever a co-chair of the Shalom Bayit campaign!

Stand up if you were ever an active member in the campaign!

Stand up if you are from a foundation that supported this campaign!

Stand up if you are an elected official who supported this campaign!

Stand up if you are a union member!

Stand up if you are a congregant who supported this campaign!

Anyone who ever stood up in some way for domestic workers—stand up now!

The revelatory list of participants was designed to conclude with the entire audience on its feet, collectively cheering the passage of the Domestic Workers' Bill of Rights. It illustrated the strength of the solidarity built among DWU members and employers of domestic workers throughout the Domestic Workers' Bill of Rights campaign, as well as how DWU's work had become central to JFREJ's political commitments to antiracism and economic justice. Through the campaign to support the passage of the Domestic Workers' Bill of Rights, the Shalom Bayit campaign fought for what members described as "Jewish values" in the home while they also built a progressive, multigenerational, inclusive Jewish community through their social justice organizing efforts. Following the bill's passage, members of the Shalom Bayit campaign drew on the multigenerational progressive community that had supported the Domestic Workers' Bill of Rights to raise awareness about the new law's provisions among employers of domestic workers.

The Personal Is Political

How do you encourage people to change the way they've been doing something, especially if they've been doing it that way for years? That was the question facing Shalom Bayit campaign members following the passage of the Domestic Workers' Bill of Rights. Few employers knew what the bill contained or what it might mean in practical terms. In addition to notifying domestic workers about the new law's requirements, DWU and Shalom Bayit members knew they had to inform employers of domestic workers and convince them to adopt the bill's provisions in their own homes with the care workers they hired. To convince employers to improve hiring and employment practices inside their residences, DWU and Shalom Bayit initiated a "Know Your Responsibilities" campaign to educate domestic workers' employers about the Domestic Workers' Bill of Rights.

Perhaps most importantly, Shalom Bayit and DWU members crafted a message—"My home is someone's workplace"—to draw in employers of domestic workers and to encourage them to uphold fair labor standards in their kitchens, nurseries, bathrooms, and dens. Through collaboration with Brooklyn synagogues, the Shalom Bayit campaign "commissioned" student art inspired by their Justice in the

Figure 4.3 Image of a kitchen drawn by students during a training on domestic work advocacy.

Home message, which were then reproduced as postcards. Shalom Bayit campaign members distributed the postcards to their membership to spread the word about the campaign. In one postcard image, a middle-school student had sketched a kitchen in thin black lines. A fridge in one corner, four-person table in the center, and the sink and stove on either side created an inverse "U" shape, all penciled in with the words, "This Is Someone's Workplace," scrawled along the bottom, and "Respect All Work," written in tiny letters in the blank space of the kitchen cabinets. The student's art serves as a vivid reminder of the connections that DWU has made with allies of all ages across New York City. At the same time, the involvement of children in advocating for caretakers' rights again depicts—literally in this case—the uniquely personal aspects of caregiving as a field of employment and DWU's savviness in channeling these close connections into persuasive political alliances.

The children's artwork also literally illustrated a point that Helen had made when we last talked, explaining that "many times, the employers' homes become our office and our place of business too. . . .

We're having these conversations in our workplaces, which coincidentally happens to be the employers' homes." DWU activists and their allies did reshape the meaning of existing spaces to transform and politicize these spheres. The home became a workplace; the kitchen table a bargaining table. In this semantic and practical reframing, new spaces provide room for domestic workers who, as Helen noted, otherwise become invisible in the parks, playgrounds, and kitchens where they work.

Illustrating the role of private homes and worksites as organizational spaces, one main way members of the Shalom Bayit campaign encouraged employers to improve their practices and join in broader political and legislative activism on behalf of domestic workers' rights is through what they called "living room gatherings." As the name implies, these meetings occurred in people's private homes, transforming what we may think of as private spaces into political spaces for education and organizing to support domestic workers. Shalom Bayit campaign members had organized living room gatherings for years in support of the passage of the Domestic Workers' Bill of Rights, hosting individuals who employed nannies, home health aides, and housekeepers. During the campaign to pass the Domestic Workers' Bill of Rights, living room gatherings focused on "stepups," ways that employers—in the absence of far-reaching legislation protecting this sector—could make small, manageable, and concrete changes in their employment practices to move closer to the ethical standard of employment espoused by Shalom Bayit campaign members. Identifying these small steps was significant because, as an Employers for Justice organizer explained to me, "Many employers are overwhelmed by the idea of changing all practices at once, so it's easier to think about steps, and these are guidelines to allow people to engage at whatever level they think they can." These steps included offering paid vacation leave, compensation for travel time to and from work, reimbursement for on-the-job meals, overtime pay, and establishing a written contract that outlines job duties, termination procedures, and annual pay increases.

During these meetings, employers of domestic workers discussed some of the issues they faced—such as how to navigate workers' compensation insurance for in-home workers or whether to pay "on the books"—while members of the Shalom Bayit campaign used the meetings to encourage employers to support the Domestic Workers' Bill of Rights and to consider offering transportation pay, sick time, and paid vacation to the domestic workers they employed. Following the passage of the Domestic Workers' Bill of Rights, living room gatherings shifted focus to educating employers about the law's stipulations and to supporting employers as they implemented the law in their private homes. In addition, employer activists in the Shalom Bayit campaign had to contend with the discrepancy between what activists urged employers to do and the far less rigorous demands of the new law.

In 2012, I attended one of these living room gatherings with Shalom Bayit campaign members. At this meeting, a half dozen of us were all seated in what would have likely been referred to in previous eras as a "drawing room" of a typical Park Slope brownstone in Brooklyn. Crisp, clean, and inviting, it had a couch, a couple of upholstered chairs, a low coffee table, and an unused fireplace with a bare mantel. I typed feverishly, courtroom-stenographer style, on the laptop balanced between my knees while I sat uncomfortably on an ottoman. Others were seated to my left and right, forming a tight circle. Each person introduced herself and explained her connection to care work. A Shalom Bayit campaign member to my right said that she was in attendance because "the personal is political." Another explained that she employed a part-time babysitter to care for her two school-age children. Another said she had hired a full-time nanny many years ago, while two others reported that they paid a housekeeper to clean their homes on a weekly basis.

While most of the Shalom Bayit campaign members were themselves employers of nannies, housekeepers, and eldercare givers, there was a smaller group of activists in their twenties who were not employers of domestic workers themselves but who organized the group, having more available time to strategize and plan alongside DWU members than many of the older Shalom Bayit members. These younger activists held monthly planning meetings, liaised with DWU by attending DWU's coalition meetings, set up informational tables outside of Saturday services and during Purim parties to recruit employers to join the group, and even taught workshops for children about the value of domestic labor during Hebrew classes.

I spent much of my time observing this smaller group of activists from the Shalom Bayit campaign during their meetings, recruitment activities, and trainings. While they identified many motivations for their activism on behalf of domestic workers, they each shared with me that working in coalition with DWU allowed them to enact their political values, which included fighting against economic exploitation, racism, and anti-immigrant policies, and fighting on behalf of a feminized workforce. One young woman recalled that both her grandmother and mother identified as feminists, and that they had instilled in her a skepticism about media representations of women, particularly advertising. During college, she told me, she and other feminists "spent a lot of time talking politics and talking patriarchy, White patriarchy and Black patriarchy," broadening her analysis to consider how race in particular and class by extension complicate universal ideas of sisterhood among women.

Reflecting on her political priorities, another activist told me that racial justice "was my first major issue. But I think domestic work is a place where it meets class, gender oppression, [and] immigration rights." In my conversations with the young activists behind the Shalom Bayit campaign, I was struck by how their motivations reflected the early insights of antiracist, feminist scholars like Judith Rollins (1985, 3), who described domestic work as the meeting point of "the capitalist class structure, the patriarchal sex structure, and the racial division of labor." Rollins's analysis and its embodiment in the activism of Shalom Bayit campaign members reflect another aspect of DWU's community unionism—their work to identify and connect systemic issues that unite us in struggles for a more just society. Shalom Bayit's activism showcased their commitment to addressing these issues through their collaboration with DWU.

At a small Shalom Bayit campaign planning meeting in Washington Heights, for example, two group members and I spent nearly an hour discussing how people talk about hiring someone to work in their home. The grammatical construction commonly used by domestic worker employers at that time was, "We *have* a nanny" or "*our* housekeeper." For example, a *New York Times* article on domestic workers opened with the line, "If you're lucky enough to *have* a nanny" (Sullivan 2015). This language reinforces perceptions of superiority, devaluing the professionalism of home-based workers. Shalom

Bayit campaign members pointed out that saying one "has" a nanny or housekeeper implies ownership and with it the racist presumptions of American slavery. Not only that, they explained to one another and to me, saying that someone "has" a domestic worker obscures—or hides—the employment arrangement between these two parties. The only sensible alternative, we concluded, was to encourage employers of domestic workers to use the verb *to employ* (and its synonyms). To re-write the *New York Times* article as "If you're lucky enough to *employ* a nanny" is both a lexically clear and accurate description of the employment relationship that Shalom Bayit promotes among members.

This focus on crafting equitable language to describe the do-mestic work relationship was not trivial for Shalom Bayit campaign members. It reflected the group's broader objective of persuading employers of domestic workers to refer to themselves as such. For these Shalom Bayit campaign activists as well as domestic workers, the employer-employee relationship is a critical terrain in the fight for domestic worker justice. Given the historic lack of labor laws and the difficulty of enforcing laws in private homes, employers must proactively adopt better employment practices in their own homes. Encouraging employers to see the nannies, housekeepers, and home healthcare workers they employ as employees is a critical first step. As one Shalom Bayit campaign member explained, "One of the problems is that, because domestic work is not valued as real work, oftentimes employers of domestic workers fail to see themselves as employers." When domestic work employers adopt the label of *employer*, this en-courages the recognition that domestic work is "real work" and it forces employers to confront their employment practices directly.

Debates and discomfort over titles and terms—even for Shalom Bayit campaign members themselves—stood as proxies for employ-ers' uneasiness in acting as "bosses" in their homes. As evidence of the obstacles working group members faced in convincing the fami-lies who employ domestic workers that they are, in fact, employers, the host of our living room gathering explained that she felt "the boss title was too formal" since she had largely employed part-time baby-sitters. Shalom Bayit campaign members regarded the uneasiness of identifying as an employer as an organizing barrier, preventing those employing babysitters, nannies, or personal attendants from formal-izing wages, hours, and work duties.

Part of this discomfort with the term *employer*, for many people, comes from a disidentification with those wealthy elite who hire a full household staff. It signals a conscious attempt to distance themselves from salient cultural depictions of wealthy, cloistered women of yesteryear with whom Employers for Justice members do not share a political ideology or class status. To employers, employing a part-time babysitter, hiring a cleaning service, or negotiating Medicare and private insurance company bureaucracy to provide in-home care and assistance for an elderly parent do not closely resemble the employment practices of elite New Yorkers who may employ a household staff. Shalom Bayit campaign members typically were not from the ranks of the very elite; instead, they were usually from dual-income families who hired domestic workers in an attempt to balance career, nuclear and extended family, and household responsibilities. They sought to remake seemingly apolitical relational and employment practices through a social justice lens. Shalom Bayit campaign members utilized the diversity of experiences among employers to recruit politically conscious and sympathetic participants to attend meetings and take on leadership roles. For these mostly middle-class employers, the act of identifying themselves as an employer was a step toward formalizing the domestic work relationship, countering the personalism of household labor that has historically disadvantaged workers.

Kitchen Table Dialogues: Transforming Spaces and Employment Practices

Explaining the success of the Domestic Workers' Bill of Rights campaign, a longtime employer-activist proudly stated:

> This began, for me, when I started employing a nanny. I wanted it to be based on a sense of mutual respect and tranquility in the home. Jews for Racial and Economic Justice began discussions, and the first goal was to support DWU in their effort to lobby the city council to get the employee agency to start informing employers of nannies' rights.

This employer-activist explained that while legislating labor rights was an imperfect solution, it offered the clearest path to protecting the women employed in the care sector while also preserving the possibility of attaining fuller protections through a union contract:

> We figured it was a long shot for any attention in Albany due [to] its historic exclusions in the Labor Relations Act. The only recourse was to ask that rights be legislated, and the package could mimic a union contract. The bill went into effect in fall 2010, and this was the first state legislation. It sets a national precedent.... This is a story of success starting in living rooms.

This employer-activist's summation, that "this is a story of success starting in living rooms," powerfully emphasized the efficacy of the home as the site of transformation and of politics.

The meeting's host then asked those gathered, "Can we engage in dialogues or negotiations that would lead to standards, and more households doing the same thing, setting a higher standard?" The host was gauging employers' interest in joining a pilot effort to broach negotiations between domestic workers and their employers. DWU and Shalom Bayit campaign members planned to begin what they called the Kitchen Table Dialogues (originally named the Domestic Justice Zone project). "Right now, it's still the Park Slope phase and we changed it to 'the Kitchen Table Dialogues' just to make it a little homier," Helen updated me when we last spoke nearly a decade ago. Unlike the Living Room Gatherings, in which employers met to discuss how to improve their own hiring practices and support DWU's efforts, Kitchen Table Dialogues included domestic workers as well as employers of domestic workers coming together to discuss both points of disagreement and points of collaboration.

These dialogues mimicked the kinds of bargaining that workers organized in a union would undertake with their employers in another industry. As I noted in Chapter 2, the New York State Labor Relations Act prohibits domestic workers from collectively bargaining or officially negotiating like a union would, a relic of race-based legal exclusions of the New Deal laws. The idea behind the Kitchen Table Dialogues was simple: Could domestic workers and employers of domestic workers come together to explore issues such as fair wages, hours, job responsibilities, severance pay, payroll taxes, and respect in the home/workplace? It was an ambitious plan given the specifics of the domestic work sector. First, gathering dispersed domestic workers from across the city each with a different employer presented many logistical and practical challenges. And, second, the unwillingness of employers of nannies, home healthcare workers, and housekeepers to think of themselves as bosses presented a strategic and psychological obstacle to convincing employers to engage in something like a union negotiation.

Yet, the image of a union-style negotiation resonated with DWU members as they envisioned these dialogues. Meva told me:

> My understanding is that we are going to sit at one table. On this side is going to be domestic workers and on this side parents and people from [Employers for Justice]. I don't know if it's going to be that way or it's going to be mixed up. I don't know why I visualize it like that.

Meva's image conveys the idea of two sides debating, perhaps disagreeing, and exploring critical issues together. She continued, "I think we need to listen to them, to what the employers want. Then they want to hear what we want, and then it's going to be hopefully a nice conversation. That's my feeling." Meva noted that her goals for these dialogues are "hopefully to raise the standards, like to have the two weeks of vacation pay, sick day pay, and personal days."

At the end of these dialogues, the planners expected to have an employment agreement they could share across New York City's neighborhoods. The initiative would establish a voluntary, neighborhood-based, domestic work employment contract. The groups hope to eventually convince individual families to adopt the terms of the contract in private hiring, wage, and job scope decisions, essentially standardizing the terms of employment for all domestic workers in the area. The initiative demonstrates the power of community unionism by achieving for domestic workers through voluntary collective action and savvy alliances what New York State labor laws do not afford them: the right to bargain collectively with their employers.

Like recruiting care workers in their isolated and dispersed workplaces to join DWU, engaging employers has been a slow and intensive process. During these Kitchen Table Dialogues, employers reported feeling uncertain about employment norms and unaware of new laws. Online parenting groups attempt to demystify this employment relationship, and private therapists even specialize in treating the emotional stress it causes wealthy employers (Sullivan 2015). Shalom Bayit campaign members attempted to counter this isolation by creating what they call *culture shift*: changing the perceptions that employers have of hiring domestic workers.

I spoke casually with several families who employed nannies and housekeepers and who had heard of or attended Living Room Gatherings with the Shalom Bayit campaign. While not members of JFREJ or a part of the Shalom Bayit campaign, they reported that the Living Room Gatherings were a useful source of information and motivation to consider the ethical implications of hiring a domestic worker. One woman described her attendance as "eye-opening," causing her to think of herself as an employer with legal obligations to the childcare provider she employed. More politically minded Shalom Bayit campaign members also regarded these opportunities to discuss their employment practices as personally meaningful, as they gave families, working parents, and activists the occasion to enact their political convictions and religious values through small changes in their mundane work-balance routines and to marry these micropractices to statewide and national organizing efforts. Shalom Bayit campaign members have also been dynamic additions to national and statewide organizing, including national events like the Care Congress I describe in the next section, bringing large swaths of care workers and allied groups together to maintain momentum following the passage of the Domestic Workers' Bill of Rights.

Building Solidarity through Narrative and Emotion

One Sunday in the summer of 2012, I entered a large gymnasium already filled with hundreds of domestic workers, labor activists, disability rights activists, and advocates for the elderly. Unlike other citywide events I had participated in and researched, I knew only a handful of attendees. Most of the familiar faces I saw were on the platform at the far end of the gym, delivering remarks and scuttling back and forth as microphones changed hands and speakers took the podium. I sat in the back where JFREJ members took turns recording the event in shifts before joining a handful of DWU members whom

I recognized and who were sitting on folding chairs in the audience. The Sunday afternoon crowd had assembled for New York's first and the nation's largest Care Congress, organized by Caring Across Generations, a coalition led by the National Domestic Workers Alliance and labor unions to take the victory of New York's Domestic Workers' Bill of Rights national; the event was promoted on the Caring Across Generations website as "a town hall dialogue designed to build quality and dignity care for all" (Caring Across Generations). Mary, one of the event's organizers and a longtime labor union leader, proclaimed, "We're here today because we believe that those in our society who care for those who are most vulnerable—our family members—and allow them to live with dignity at the very end of their lives should at least be given the opportunity to have some dignity in their own lives as well."

Reflecting the central role of storytelling to the domestic worker justice movement, Care Congresses from Seattle to Texas have encouraged participants to "share their care stories," uniting a novel constituency of providers and recipients, grant organizations, and traditional labor unions. Poo (2010, n.p.) writes:

> We knew that the stories and leadership of domestic workers would be a driving force throughout the campaign. What we didn't expect was how many other people would feel that their own life stories were so closely connected to the stories of domestic workers.

Stories are an especially powerful tactic for motivating involvement in campaigns for justice and equality—an insight that DWU members and their national collaborators recognized. Narrative played a role in all the public events I attended with DWU members. The purpose of sharing domestic work narratives reflects the observation by linguistic anthropologists Elinor Ochs and Lisa Capps (1996, 22) that "each . . . narrative situated in time and space engages only facets of a narrator's . . . selfhood in that it evokes only certain memories, concerns, or expectations." By evoking memories, concerns, and expectations that advance the rights of and protections for domestic workers, activists in DWU and their allies selectively and savvily used narratives and storytelling as a way to achieve political goals.

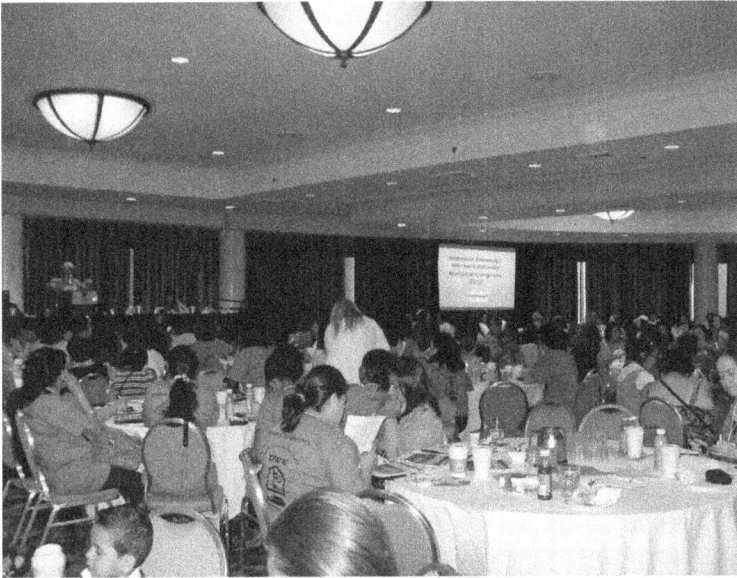

Figure 4.4 Image of domestic workers gathered in a large banquet hall during the 2012 National Domestic Workers Alliance Convention.

At a leadership meeting I attended in February 2012, domestic workers and employers of domestic workers discussed how best to inform people about the Domestic Workers' Bill of Rights' passage, while also lamenting its limitations in private homes where nannies and caretakers work. "We need to think about what stories we should be telling," one woman suggested. In small groups, we began to consider how best to tell "narratives of the Bill of Rights campaign." "Which elements will make a great story?" the same woman inquired, and then added, "Which narratives will help us meet our goals?" This approach to narrative demonstrates how domestic work activists consciously craft stories that will resonate with others and motivate others to action, illustrating the genre's ability to incite, connect, and inspire. And it showcases how integral it has been for organizing workers and their allies in the domestic work sector.

Care Congresses marshalled the longstanding emphasis on narratives of care within the global domestic workers' movement. In her research on the passage of the 2011 International Labour Organization's Convention concerning Decent Work for Domestic Workers, Jennifer Fish (2017, 152) finds that "no other movement has used personal storytelling to this extent." Fish argues that, in this context, "domestic workers used their personal experiences of suffering in making their emotional appeals" (149). Along with calls for dignity and respect for care workers, she argues that these narrative tactics are effective tools for "moral and collective persuasion" (148). In Care Congresses and other New York City activist events, narratives similarly act as persuasive tools, particularly through their power to unite disparate groups of people through shared emotional experiences.

Sharing stories at these types of events extends beyond the audience-orator dynamic. In this case, the audience members each shared their own care stories with one another as well. In my group, three of us discussed our paid work as child- and eldercare providers, and discussed how we anticipate needing care and assistance as we age. "I am a homecare worker but will also need care within the next five years," one woman explained. This political form of engagement through highly personal, emotive speech acts—narrative, sharing, giving voice, telling *your* care story—has been incredibly successful in building a movement with a precedent-setting national impact.

DWU's emphasis on personal narrative further conditions the activists involved—workers and employers alike—to rely on evocative, affective speech to build rapport and to empower one another. The Care Congress itself—pitched in explicitly affective terms (including the event title and frequent references to *emotion*, *care*, and *love*) and through staged participatory narrative events that encourage attendees to "share their care stories"—was organized entirely around a series of speakers who shared their stories of caring for others. One of the most powerful stories came from Judy, a longtime activist-employer with the Shalom Bayit campaign:

> Domestic workers have been part of my life for as long as I can remember. When my mother went back to work, a caregiver cared for me until I started kindergarten. Her manner was rough, sometimes fierce. I always knew that she was entirely devoted to me and I adored her. Fast forward: My son was eighteen months old when my husband and I hired a caregiver for him so I could return to work. . . . Fast forward again

to more recent times: Everyone is getting older. Every other Wednesday, Sally comes to clean our apartment. On the alternate Wednesday, she cleans my mother-in-law's apartment, not far from ours. My mother-in-law, called "Gran" by everyone in the family, is ninety-four and completely self-sufficient. She shops, pays her bills, balances her checkbook, takes the bus to the beauty parlor, and meets her friends for lunch. Then Gran is almost completely self-sufficient most of the time. Sometimes Sally needs to help her get out of the bathtub, to keep her medication straight, walk to the supermarket. In small but important ways, Sally is filling in by expanding her job description. We are worried sick about a thousand things. . . . Where would we find someone with the vision to understand Gran's enormous personal pride, her independence? Well, it worked out, Jane entered the picture, and Gran relaxed and allowed herself to be cared for. A real respect developed between the two women. Gran lived another five years to ninety-nine, and Jane became the person who knew her, who could . . . read her body and her spirit. On the last morning it was not the doctor, not another family member, it was Jane who called to suggest that we come over. She sensed that something was changing. . . . I'm part of Caring Across Generations because I believe that we're all in this together. . . . Our job is to make stories like mine, lucky ones with happy endings, the standard, the norm, no longer the exception.

Judy's narrative reinforced a definition of caregiving as "a defining moral practice. . . . of empathetic imagination, responsibility, witnessing, and solidarity with those in great need" (Kleinman 2009, 293), as is DWU's organizing and activism. The caring relationships that develop between paid caregivers and the children, adults, and families for whom they work entail mutual respect; Jane's ability to read subtle cues, and to sense when "something was changing," allowed Gran to remain as self-sufficient as possible. The audience members who worked as elderly companions and home health aides could recognize themselves in this story, as well as the respect that Judy and Gran had for Jane, making the story also a tribute to care workers' professional patience, persistence, and compassion.

Judy's narrative reflects the campaign's central tenet—namely, that care is necessary from cradle to grave and, in the current socio-economic climate, the care available in the United States is often *paid* care. Through the collective act of sharing stories, care work narratives are used to make change. "Our job," as Judy said, "is to make stories like mine . . . the standard." Judy's story ultimately deploys the personalism of domestic work to argue for broadly redistributive policies that would benefit care workers and recipients of care alike. And, ironically, in its romanticizing of domestic work's "personal relations of service," Judy's narrative illuminates the tension in how DWU and its allies use personalism to build solidarity, since the personalism of the sector has roots in the "one of the family trope" historically used by employers to obscure the labor of enslaved and indentured women (Romero 1992).

Yet, activists at this and other events reinforced this notion of caring in their affective communicative strategies and emotive personal narratives, allowing them to leverage the implicit affect and morality of Judy's narrative. Scholars have noted the central role that emotion and affect play in political activism. Sociologists Jeff Goodwin, James Jasper, and Francesca Polletta (2001, 2) write that "until the 1960s emotions were considered a key . . . to understanding virtually all political action." Jasper (2011, 292) further explains that activists "arouse and display . . . emotions as a way to get things done. . . . Organizers try to arouse emotions to attract new recruits, sustain the commitment and the discipline of those already in a movement, and persuade outsiders." Poo (2010, n.p.) has similarly argued that DWU's activism "provides a hopeful push—despite the unknown—toward campaigns based on love, to bring us into the right relationships with one another for the change we need." Indeed, domestic workers and their allies aroused and displayed emotion in collective settings like Care Congresses to overcome the isolation of their dispersed jobs and to build solidarity with one another. Drawing on the personalism of care work, DWU members build on the emotion, love, and connection of care work to establish enduring coalitions and to draw others into their movement.

The stated aim of Care Congresses—to build a care economy—requires participants, storytellers like Judy, and organizers to emotionally establish a collective or a shared political sensibility to support legislative goals and sustain participation long enough to realize their objectives. At Care Congresses, and other events that bring together care workers and their diverse allies to unite in a vision for a new type of economy and a new type of society, care as an ideal or a principle emerges. It emerges from the embodied labor, storytelling performances, and politics of diverse domestic workers and activists who created a political movement based on their care. When we consider care as "shared risk," as Christina Sharpe (2018) does, the politics of care workers and their allies assume even greater urgency and importance.

5

"We'll Roll Out"

*Acts of Care and Solidarity following the Passage
of the Domestic Workers' Bill of Rights*

At 5:45 A.M., the avenues that frame Union Square were empty.
Starbucks, Dunkin' Donuts, and Pret A Manger had not yet
opened their doors to early-morning clientele. I stood at the
corner of Seventeenth Street and Broadway, sheltered by the entryway
of a Barnes & Noble that has since closed. I faced the park's pavilion,
two playgrounds, and the northern entrances for the four, five, and
six subway lines. Lights emanated from Whole Foods, Filene's Basement, Forever 21, Best Buy, and Nordstrom Rack along the park's
southern border. Union Square is now ensconced among wealthy
Manhattan neighborhoods, New York University's northern bound-
ary, high-rise apartment buildings, and corporate big box retailers.
However, back in 1882, before its commercial facelift, Union Square
hosted the nation's first Labor Day parade, earning a historic land-
mark designation in 1997. On this October morning in 2010, thousands of labor activists from the tristate area renewed the park's early
labor-oriented spirit. They planned to use the location as a meeting
spot where activists could board buses for the One Nation Working
Together Rally in Washington, DC. I waited for a contingent of DWU
members I was joining for the rally.

We were about thirty-five in all that October morning: mostly
DWU members and staff, all Caribbean women, and three White

U.S.-born female interns. We had all arrived before 6 A.M. to embark on the drive down to the capital. We watched the city awaken. Garbage trucks and taxis completing their red-eye shifts hummed along the main arteries as the Union Square perimeter swelled with other groups of protestors on their way to the rally and with workers en route to early-morning gigs. When the bus didn't arrive as planned, our two bus captains, Jean and Helen, paced up and down Seventeenth Street, fielding calls from partner organizations, trying to locate the errant bus.

Because I spent many months volunteering inside DWU before I began conducting interviews, I sometimes cannot recall the exact moment when I met one of its members. It often feels as though I have always known these activists. But I clearly remember the women I met who gathered for the rally. It was the first of many road trips I took with DWU, and I was anxious and alert with my notebook in hand, self-consciously introducing myself to everyone who arrived. The day itself was etched into my memory as one of those events where everything that could go wrong, including losing a bus, did. It was my introduction to the group's perseverance and it framed my admiration of many of the women activists whose words I recount in this book.

Unlike the dozens of DWU-sponsored trips to the state's capital over the previous years, the One Nation Working Together rally was a national event, sponsored by the National Democratic Party and a cadre of labor unions. One of DWU's union partners had arranged transportation. But demand outpaced capacity and local bus companies were unable to accommodate the thousands of protestors coming from across the Northeast. Our small group fell through cracks. So, we waited, uncertain about the cause of the delay or if we would even make the trip. One of the other interns suggested that we give up and head home. Other members grumbled about the October chill, as many of us had dressed for Washington, DC's warmer weather. Every so often, as the chilly crowd began to grumble and complain, a member's voice would counter biblically, "Thank God for today, it's a day that God has made," dissipating our burgeoning irritability.

By 9 A.M., noticing the group's restlessness, the DWU food committee sprang into action, pulling out breakfast provisions that they prepared and packed for our bus trip. They set up a sidewalk buffet of empanadas and warm beverages right there on Seventeenth Street. This impromptu meal was my initial encounter with the welcoming generosity of the DWU membership, enacted through preparing and sharing food with all in attendance, regardless of length of time within the organization, familiarity with the other members, or role with the group. A rotating cohort of DWU members prepared, packed, and transported home-cooked meals for the full membership at this and every subsequent action and event I attended. Even when participation swelled into the hundreds, small cans of Sterno kept trays of fish, chicken, and vegetables warm during hours of debate, performance, voting, and strategizing. These seemingly small acts of hospitality and care—preparing and providing food at each event and meeting—offer a glimpse into the daily working of DWU's solidarity politics.[1]

In the previous chapter, I described the power that DWU built through their alliances with workers in other industries and employers of domestic workers. In this chapter, I describe some of the day-to-day experiences of care, camaraderie, and unity that occurred during DWU meetings, sustaining meaningful bonds among workers and collectively contextualizing their concerns and experiences. I also describe how domestic workers use solidarity protests on behalf of abused and exploited domestic workers to forge connections that can overcome the isolation of domestic work jobs, empower and deepen workers' commitment, and spur them to action. These solidarity protests are a part of DWU's campaign called "Justice for Exploited Domestic Workers," which they describe as one aspect of their advocacy work, and which, I argue, epitomizes the solidarity approach that the organization uses to enforce workplace protections. The campaign targets individual employers for specific instances of illegal behavior, using both protests and legal tactics, to publicize egregious incidents of abuse and mistreatment and to seek financial recompense for aggrieved workers. I focus on the solidarity that this campaign engenders and its ramifications for other domestic workers I interviewed and protested alongside who said that these events empowered them and illustrated DWU's collective power.

First, to illustrate the difference that political solidarity can make in how domestic workers understand an event, I begin this chapter by discussing the details of a Guinean housekeeper named Nafissatou Diallo's sexual assault by a prominent French politician. Diallo's case drew international attention and crystalized many of the issues facing domestic workers in New York City, including on-the-job abuse, harassment, and racism. To draw out the implications of DWU's solidarity at meetings and during protests, I contrast how DWU members discussed Diallo's case with how Fatou, an unaffiliated care worker, interpreted the same situation. To contextualize Fatou's individual impression of Diallo's case, I also delve into a discussion of some of the racist harassment that she, and other immigrant women of color, experienced in New York City—an influential and devastating aspect of many domestic workers' lives. By juxtaposing Fatou's interpretation of Diallo's case against DWU members' interpretations, this chapter illuminates how the trainings and support DWU members were routinely exposed to helped buoy their sense of solidarity not only with one another but with Diallo—a high-profile stranger with whom they could empathize.

Expressing Care and Solidarity during DWU Meetings

I was staffing the phones in the DWU office in May 2011, when Diallo, a thirty-two-year-old Guinean housekeeper employed by the Times Square luxury hotel Sofitel, brought sexual assault charges against Dominique Strauss-Kahn, a French politician and then director of the International Monetary Fund. Several media outlets called DWU for a reaction to the news. Strauss-Kahn was a high-profile figure, and Diallo's charges received more coverage than similar crimes committed against individual domestic workers employed in private homes. Suddenly, the normally hidden abuse of isolated women working in homes, hotels, hospitals, and nursing facilities appeared daily on the front page of newspapers and dominated the conversations I had with DWU members and other care workers.

The ubiquitous media coverage frequently targeted Diallo herself. Tabloid outlets, most prominently the *New York Post*, ran salacious headline after salacious headline, accusing Diallo of working as a prostitute and of setting up Strauss-Kahn for blackmail. The hotel also released card swipe logs that documented exactly where Diallo was in the hotel. Some news outlets claimed these records undermined her account of the assault. Although there was irrefutable physical evidence of a sexual interaction between Strauss-Kahn and Diallo, prosecutors dropped the charges, citing a series of inconsistencies in Diallo's reported biographical details.

Here I describe the abuse and injustice that Diallo's case unearthed, the distrust and sensational media coverage that attended it, and DWU members' reactions to it. The case exemplifies how racism affects many DWU members and domestic workers in New York City. Anthropologist Leith Mullings (2005, 684) defines racism in this way, highlighting its relationality:

> Racism is a relational concept. It is a set of practices, structures, beliefs, and representations that transforms certain forms of perceived differences, generally regarded as indelible and unchangeable, into inequality. It works through modes of dispossession, which have included subordination, stigmatization, exploitation, exclusion, various forms of physical violence, and sometimes genocide. It is . . . interwoven with other forms of inequality, particularly class, gender, sexuality, and nationality.

As we will see, the intimacy of domestic workers' roles inside private homes exposes them to racist abuse and harassment on the job, but racism also extends into their nonworking lives. In addition, most domestic workers in New York City are immigrants, representing nearly 80 percent of the city's caregivers according to a National Domestic Workers Alliance analysis of 2019 census data (National Domestic Workers Alliance, n.d.).

Diallo was in the United States as a refugee and her immigration status frequently came up in coverage of her case. Prosecutors apparently uncovered inconsistencies between the narrative she gave during her initial immigration hearing and her recollection of the same events, years later, during her questioning on the rape accusations. Some feared that Diallo might be deported as a result of bringing charges against Strauss-Kahn, but she was not, despite threats of deportation and detention circulating in the media at this time. The *New York Times* published an article on Diallo's case based on interviews in New York and across the Atlantic among Diallo's family members, under the headline, "From Hut in Africa to the Glare of a High Profile Assault Case" (Barnard, Nossiter, and Semple 2011). This headline traffics in antiquated stereotypes and rhetorical framings that collapse the fifty-four nations on the African continent into a single entity. Such stereotypes constitute—or make up—one aspect of the process of *racialization*, a term social scientists use to refer to the processes by which racial meanings become attached to individuals, groups, social practices, and systems of power. The Diallo case also exemplifies journalistic Orientalism, an enduring issue in describing groups of people from around the world. Social theorist Edward Said (1978) coined the term *Orientalism* to characterize how "Western" scholars write about cultures from Asia, the Middle East, and North Africa. These representations, he argues, are exaggerated clichés stemming from imperialism. The *New York Times* headline, by substituting the term "hut" for Diallo's particular experiences, reinforces an idea of Diallo's country of origin as an "unchanging abstraction" (Said 1978, 16).

Later that summer, I sat around a rectangular conference table in DWU's Herald Square office with a small group of domestic workers as we concluded a two-day training. It had been a long, hot weekend and I expected everyone to disperse as soon as the training ended. But news of Diallo's case came up and we all remained at the table to discuss it. A longtime domestic worker gave us an update on the news: prosecutors planned to drop the charges against Strauss-Kahn, despite the presence of physical evidence. Her revelation elicited a range of responses from the domestic workers present. Their reactions illustrated to me just how common some elements of Diallo's experience were: the sense of being watched while at work (as with her card swipes) and in public (as in the headlines), the worry that one's immigration status could be contested, and the shared experience of not being believed by one's employer and others holding positions of power in New York.

Shirley, a South Asian nanny, observed that "her [Diallo's] dialect took them days to interpret" and asked, "How do we know how much is accurate?" Kay, who had lived in New York for a decade "without a green card," as she put it, declared, "She's going to get deported. They have dropped the charges against Strauss." The other women concurred, expressing concern over reports that Diallo's refugee status had been jeopardized as a result of her contradictory accounts. She has "bad papers," one woman observed. Pamela laughed nervously as she interjected, "People don't understand the surveillance." She cautioned the others, "Every move, every call. It's all computerized at that hotel." Pamela was referencing the discrepancies that emerged in Diallo's accounts of events and the data captured by her employers' card-entry system. Pamela's sentiment reflected her own experiences in New York City working for multiple employers, and her own pervasive sense of being watched and tracked. In her research with Brooklyn nannies, sociologist Tamara Mose Brown (2011, 58) also found that nannies reported a sense of surveillance in public spaces, like playgrounds and libraries, where other childcare providers and parents may notice, record, and publish reports of nannies' perceived indiscretions online to parenting groups and similar sites about parenting.

Shirley, the longtime activist, chimed in again, challenging a tabloid column's insinuation that Diallo was a pathological liar: "If you're in shock, it's a normal reaction. I've seen it in other trauma cases. They [traumatized victims of sexual assault and rape] change stories all the time." Kay agreed, saying, "It's how society makes you feel when you are an immigrant. It's the [process of applying for a] green card." "That story [one tells when applying for refugee status] needs to be consistent till you die," she said frankly, adding, "When you are Black and you are an immigrant, you have to tell that story till you die." When I recall Kay's words, I can imagine the high level of stress and pressure that such scrutiny must entail. The exchange among these domestic workers—all women of color, all immigrants—reveals the fears that they live with on a daily basis in New York City, resulting not only from the precarity of their jobs but also their potential exposure to racist harassment or violence from working alone in someone's private home, and in many cases, their undocumented immigration status.

For this small, multicultural group of immigrant domestic workers and advocates, the Diallo case epitomized many of the bureaucratic hoops they had to jump through themselves for papers, jobs, apartments, and so on. What particularly resonated was the recognition that they too could be misunderstood, or deemed fraudulent, undocumented, or "bad" in some legally damaging way. *Could I also have bad papers or a bad job?* Citing the dual pressures of antiblack racism and anti-immigrant sentiment and legislation, the women participating in this small training rendered in practical terms the broader issues structuring the Strauss-Kahn case and its media coverage: the realities of racism and sexism, punitive U.S. immigration policy, and the abuse and exploitation that domestic workers encounter. Anthropologist Faye Harrison (1995, 59) argues that "racial meanings and hierarchies are unstable . . . but constrained by relatively constant white supremacy and the black subordination that demarcates the social bottom." This persistent and damaging hierarchy is the larger context that shapes DWU members' migratory and labor experiences. When Diallo's case splashed the hidden abuses that domestic workers of color endure on the front page of newspapers, the reservoir of injustices that immigrant women in New York City endure surfaced along with it. Inside DWU meeting rooms, domestic workers provided solidarity and support to one another, listening to each other share their reactions to the Diallo case and its implications for their own lives.

In addition to spending time with women at DWU, I also established relationships with West African immigrant women who I interviewed about their migration and care work experiences. In considering how some of the West African women I interviewed responded to Diallo's case, I was struck by the absence of solidarity—and the pervasive sense of fear and distrust that replaced it.[2] Around the time when Diallo's story broke, for example, I was spending many days per week with another care worker, Fatou, who was not affiliated with DWU. Fatou had worked as a home health aide earlier in her career and returned to work out of financial desperation in 2012, despite the chronic and nearly debilitating knee pain she cited as her reason for retiring.

I was riding in the back seat of Fatou's white minivan one afternoon, a common occurrence. I fumbled with the child-locked automatic windows, as her husband Mamadou wove through the traffic on the West Side Highway toward his midtown dialysis treatment facility. Sitting beside him in the front seat, Fatou instructed me to leave the window alone and used her controls to lower the one closest to me. "Thank you," I sighed, before returning to typing up notes on my proto-Smartphone to capture our conversation. Mamadou glared at me through the rearview mirror, assuming I was sending a text message, and chided me: "Finish texting. I'll wait. This is important." It was not uncommon for Mamadou to signal to me that I should pay close attention before he spoke, as he did on this afternoon.

"I'm typing our conversation into my phone, so I won't forget," I explained, trying to appease Mamadou. Fatou asked me, speaking about Diallo, "Do you know the maid? The maid from Guinea? I knew she was lying." Later that same afternoon, as Fatou and I sat in her parked van waiting for her husband, she repeated herself, "The maid was lying. I knew it all along." Visibly distressed, Fatou cited the *New York Post* coverage, claiming that Strauss-Kahn's viability as a French presidential candidate had made him a target for libel and slander. In an attempt to avoid a tight election, his opponent probably put Diallo up to it, she concluded. She then confided, "Liars like that give other Africans a bad name; they make it harder for us." Fatou's dismissal of Diallo can be attributed to several factors. As her concluding phrase makes clear, Fatou believed that the Diallo case jeopardized her and her family. Life in New York City was difficult for Fatou, as it was for many other women of color and immigrant women. I spent countless hours by Fatou's side, throughout the five boroughs and later in Mali when we visited her family members for a wedding. For Fatou, migrating to the United States, a prospect that once promised upward mobility and ease had turned out to be arduous, physically depleting, financially insecure, and rife with ongoing, racist harassment. By drawing attention to the hidden abuse endured by immigrant women and by raising doubts about the asylum process, Diallo's case might worsen the situation for other refugees and asylum seekers, or spur condemnation of Fatou and her family. Her experiences in New York had already demonstrated that things were difficult. She worried that the Diallo case would only "make it harder for us," as would the anti-African racism that Fatou anticipated would ensue.

While the isolated setting of domestic work increases the risk of racist harassment on the job, domestic workers of color also experience racist attacks when they are off the clock, as Fatou's experience illustrates. Every week for more than a year, Fatou's downstairs neighbor phoned the fire department in the middle of the night claiming there was a fire in Fatou's unit. The ordeal awoke Fatou and her family, denying them necessary sleep and causing all manner of inconvenience and risk. It persisted until a local reporter interviewed Fatou about the ongoing, unaddressed harassment. The journalist, a young Black woman, was the only person in either city government or the media who took Fatou's reports seriously; thankfully it resulted in an effective muckraking piece that shamed the police into investigating. They eventually determined that the neighbor had targeted Fatou and her family due to antiblack and anti-immigrant animus. Fatou's experience isn't uncommon. In recent years, the advent of smartphones and social media has propagated the documentation of myriad White people who use the police, or other agents of the government like the fire department, to harass people of color and especially people of African descent with potentially deadly consequences.

Racism is a form of oppression that, as Mullings points out, transforms differences into inequalities. Fatou's interpretation of the Diallo case illustrates the complexity of racialization: Fatou's distrust of Diallo demonstrates how some differences become fixed and weaponized while others are erased. Fatou worried that sharing a general geographic region and phenotypic race with Diallo would place her at greater risk in New York City. She feared Diallo's claims would "make it harder" for her and her family. Fatou's life was difficult enough, dealing with racist harassment, economic insecurity, her own injury, and her husband's illness. Like Fatou, many activists I spoke with had questions about the far-reaching implications of Strauss-Kahn's presumed innocence. *What would this mean for others who want to come forward?* But, unlike Fatou, DWU's analysis and political solidarity buoyed these activists' sense of righteous injustice at the systems of power, surveillance, and racist oppression they experienced in New York City; given this context, the Diallo case and the discussions around it thus increased their solidarity.

Through their experiences successfully lobbying for and passing the Domestic Workers' Bill of Rights, during trainings like those I described in Chapter 2, and during strategizing sessions to ensure the implementation of the Domestic Workers' Bill of Rights, DWU members recognized that their negative on-the-job experiences weren't individual but rather reflections of broader social processes. DWU's activist approach draws attention to how racism—both in the past and today—affects women in the care work sector. Identifying and historicizing the violent origins and ongoing manifestations of race-based inequalities, some aspects of which I described in Chapter 1, helped motivate DWU members to fight against them with both words and actions. Joining with other protestors, DWU activists took to the streets to insist that prosecutors press charges against Strauss-Kahn and to protest against any attempts to deport Diallo or threaten her refugee status.

"Take a Stand for Our Guinean Sister"

I attended a rally on Diallo's behalf with DWU members and their allies from the Shalom Bayit campaign[3] in July 2011. The event organizers passed out handbills that encouraged us to "take a stand for our Guinean sister, under attack. . . . Charges may be dropped as prosecutors leak adverse information on the Guinean sister, claiming 'credibility issues' over alleged misinformation on her asylum application from Guinea." The rally's emcee proclaimed, "Politics and power cannot just knock to the side a defenseless and injured Black woman while the community sits back and does nothing." This activist framing of Diallo's case explicitly marshaled the hostile treatment she received in the matrix of U.S. criminal and immigration policy to cast the system—not Diallo—as bad, as untrustworthy. As Harrison (1995) argues, racial "identities are always enacted situationally," and, in this case, those rallying in defense of Diallo made a political calculation to describe her as a Black woman, a West African woman, and as an asylee. In other words, by describing Diallo in multiple ways the organizers signaled her social location—as a housekeeper, an African immigrant, and a Black woman in the United States—and amplified the specific harm of antiblack racism and the dehumanizing state violence that Black Americans, in particular, experience.[4]

In recalling these protests for Diallo that I attended, I was struck by how the movement reflected the origins of the now viral #MeToo movement. In 2006, Tarana Burke, a Bronx native, began using the #MeToo hashtag on social media to draw attention to and stand in solidarity with women and girls who had experienced sexual assault, harassment, and abuse. This movement shared an evident overlap with the goals of DWU because of the frequent cases of abuse that domestic workers historically and currently face. "The power of Burke and others saying, 'me too,'" writes linguistic anthropologist Mariam Durrani (2018, n.p.), "pushes against the normative expectation that narratives of sexual violence are met with disbelief, denial, or rejection. Instead, #MeToo indexes believing the survivor, because the listener is also a survivor of sexual trauma." Burke's call to action had yet to hit the Hollywood zeitgeist in the summer of 2011, but it certainly encouraged activists and advocates to take sexual assault claims seriously. In 2018, after the movement made national history by encouraging survivors of sexual harassment, rape, and assault to identify with and join one another through the viral #MeToo hashtag, Ai-jen Poo, DWU's founder and the director of the National Domestic Workers Alliance, attended the Golden Globes as a guest of actress Meryl Streep, an act that publicized the advocacy work of care work activists. National domestic worker organizations have also drawn on resonances with the #BlackLivesMatter movement. Alicia Garza, who founded #BlackLivesMatter with Patrisse Cullors and Opal Tometi, is now the Special Projects Director of the National Domestic Workers Alliance, which grew out of DWU's early activism and continues to research domestic workers' workplace experiences through national surveys that support their legislative reforms.

As the #BlackLivesMatter and #MeToo movements illustrate, solidarity actions have implications beyond their immediate effect on the specific cases that generate them. We can see the efficacy of solidarity in the protests protecting Diallo from deportation, in the emergence and influence of the #BlackLivesMatter and #MeToo movements, and in DWU's protests in response to individual cases of exploited domestic workers. Critical medical anthropologist Adrienne Pine (2013, 151) introduced the concept of *somatic solidarity* to describe the complex embodied bonds she encountered among and between activist nurses and their patients during the 2009 Honduran coup, writing that "somatic solidarity . . . cannot be more than [a] fleeting process unless accompanied by ongoing collective organizing for radical social change." By rallying on Diallo's behalf and through their Justice for Exploited Domestic Workers campaign, as I describe in the next section, DWU members enacted Pine's concept of somatic solidarity, and in so doing, they demonstrated the notion that their own integrity is bound up with and dependent on their relationships to others (Dean 1996). These Justice for Exploited Domestic Workers protests, during which DWU members organized as a group to confront those responsible for another domestic worker's experience of physical assault, racist attacks, and withholding of wages, are powerful for a number of reasons—especially the solidarity that they engender among domestic workers, essential for maintaining collective presence and organizing for social change.

The Justice for Exploited Domestic Workers Campaign

On Valentine's Day 2011, along with a handful of activists from their partner organizations, DWU members gathered outside a midtown high-rise office building to protest against the former employer of a DWU member. We handed out red heart-shaped flyers that I had printed and cut out earlier that day in my volunteer role as an intern with the organization. Our valentines beseeched passersby to "have a heart" for domestic workers and included details of the employer's abusive treatment of a longtime DWU member. The DWU member had worked as a nanny for a prominent and wealthy New York family for six years, caring for their only child, "despite being grossly underpaid and mistreated," as the DWU flyer put it. DWU materials explained that "in December 2008, the employer physically assaulted and verbally abused [her] calling her a 'stupid Black b****' and said that he hated her and hoped she would die a 'horrible death'" (bowdlerization in the original).

Marching in a small circle directly outside of the employer's workplace, we intentionally disrupted business activity along the crowded midtown avenue. With amplified sound and plenty of righteous zeal, we chanted, "Up, up with domestic workers," following the cues of DWU's staff organizer. The abusive employer did not appear, but his coworkers responded as they entered and exited the building. "Let this man work. Don't you have anything better to do?" one woman asked, as she pushed between me and another protestor to enter the building's lobby. I froze, stunned by how she could dismiss her coworker's violent behavior toward another woman. Both the employer's home and workplace had been sites of DWU's direct action demonstrations for four years following the assault. Deliberately drawing attention to the often-hidden mistreatment and abuse that domestic workers endure in private homes, loud protests occurred regularly, gaining steam as the incident received coverage in a range of media outlets. Coworkers and building staff had been exposed to, and in some cases grown weary of, the noisy, confrontational tactics. But comments such as "Let him work" emphasized that the employer's level of production, rather than the abused domestic labor behind it, is what is ultimately important to many people in a capitalist society. The Justice for Exploited Workers campaign is just one leg of the multipronged organizing approach that DWU leadership advances as part of their ongoing labor rights advocacy. The campaign usually combines street-level protests, like the one on Valentine's Day 2011, with media outreach and either criminal or civil legal charges against the employers. The battles they take on garner important media coverage on the converging issues of racism, immigration policy, and labor exploitation. DWU's website explicitly recognizes this goal: "Cases raise awareness and maintain momentum around [DWU's] issues in the broader public and media" (Domestic Workers United, n.d.).

These cases provide clear examples of the forces that structure individual women's experiences of paid domestic service. In one prominent example, DWU's sister organization, Damayan, spearheaded a national movement against labor trafficking by publicly accusing U.S. Philippines Ambassador Lauro Baja individually of "modern-day slavery" and trafficking. By bringing civil charges against Baja, Damayan attacked the principle of diplomatic immunity for ambassadors, who have frequently been linked to labor trafficking of women from their respective nations. This example illustrates how publicizing individual cases can highlight the unjust and uneven working conditions experienced by many care workers. When considered alongside the Diallo case and its aftermath, the Baja case further suggests the prevalence of international elites' abuse of women workers, and the impunity granted to elite international figures by national and local governments.

This activist strategy also successfully joined the topic of compensation with solidarity politics. In an interview with *Democracy Now*'s Juan Gonzalez, Pat, a DWU activist who was abused by her employer, explained:

We work long hours, with no overtime pay. My experience, after working six-and-a-half years, never had an increase in salary, as well as no overtime pay. At times, if you work on your vacation, if you don't stand up for that vacation pay, you will not get it. You know, and it's hard at times, when you stand up for yourself, that is the time the abuse comes in. You get a verbal abuse. You get threatened with immigration [police]. And it's wrong. It's wrong.

In 2009, Pat brought a lawsuit against her employers with support from DWU and an allied legal aid agency seeking compensation for both the physical assault and for her stolen wages. The case eventually went to trial in 2012, and she received compensation for her wage theft claims.

DWU organizers remained focused on Pat's case throughout its lengthy legal process. At the 2012 Domestic Worker Convention, DWU's organizer spoke to the room of activists, eldercare providers, and immigration reform advocates about Pat's upcoming trial:

> I want to say to you that each and every one of you sitting here is the key to change. . . . One of our members, who was a nanny for over eight years and was never paid overtime for extra hours worked, was never treated with dignity and respect. Many of you sitting here know this story. Maybe all of you have been part of this fight for justice . . . from the very beginning. . . . All the love she gives to that little girl, she was paid with verbal and physical abuse. This is the time that we have to stand together and say, 'We won't take this any longer.' This has got to stop. We have to come together to create the society, one that we will not have this kind of abuse anymore. The . . . case goes to trial tomorrow, and today, as I stand here, I'm asking you to stand with us. . . . We want to show our strength and our support. . . . They've got the money; we've got the power. Who has the power?

The audience loudly responded, "We have the power!" Building on the idea of solidarity among domestic workers—the value of standing together—the organizer concluded, "Pat has been a strong voice in our organization. She has supported us and many other organizations, so I'm pleading with you: Join us outside the courthouse to support her." This appeal illustrates how the cases of individual exploited domestic workers connect to DWU's broader political goals and strategy.

The Domestic Workers' Bill of Rights campaign grew out of this employer-by-employer approach (Boris and Nadasen 2008, 467). Pat's case spanned the tail end of the Domestic Workers' Bill of Rights campaign and the immediate period after the bill passed. It was finally settled in the spring of 2012. The DWU attorney argued that awarding monetary compensation as recompense for the violence and financial exploitation that Pat experienced would signal that domestic workers deserve full and equal protection, that they deserve fairness and respect in their workplaces. The defense attorney objected to the "universalizing tone" of the remarks.

I recall standing in the back of the packed courtroom, which was filled with Pat's supporters from organizations like DWU, Damayan, Adhikaar, and Jews for Racial and Economic Justice, dumbfounded by the defense attorney's objection, particularly how he had worded it. DWU's attorney *had* used "universalizing language," as he said. But, I wondered, looking around the courtroom full of activists and immigrant domestic workers from many countries across the world, what other type of language would make sense? Dignity and respect in the workplace should be universally enjoyed. The courtroom, however, is a space dictated by legalistic speech norms and formal rules of interaction, and this tone was not permitted: the judge upheld the defense's objection. As the universalizing remarks were stricken from the record, I realized again the ongoing importance of domestic workers' willingness to support one another through solidarity protests, commiserations, and shared political goals, even against a legal system that upholds the individualism and isolation that domestic workers experience as a legal standard.

The Power of Solidarity

Beyond the individual monetary settlements awarded or the press coverage garnered, for DWU members, these public actions were more immediate and more powerful. Solidarity rallies in support of individual workers demonstrated to other DWU members that, should they find themselves in a similar situation, they would not have to face abusive and exploitative employers alone. Public protests targeting abusive employers instantiated a sense of accountability among employers and workers. When the press covered these protests, that sense of accountability spread even to those who had never encountered DWU members or their allies.

In short, this type of direct activism is empowering (Boris and Nadasen 2008). *Empowerment* is a social process that increases the political power of a community or group, or that increases individuals' power over their own lives (Bookman and Morgen 1988; Naples 1998). Some scholars have critiqued the use of *empowerment* to refer to an individual psychological process rather than a communal, political process, because the focus on individual psychology may have limited efficacy in attaining tangible improvements in people's lives (Naples 1998). Although I agree with this critique, my conversations with DWU members taught me that participating in solidary actions on behalf of other workers did have a positive psychological effect as well as—in the best cases—achieving a broader communal political outcome.

When Meva and I spoke about her first year as a DWU activist, for example, I asked about her "most powerful memory." She answered, "For me it was the first protest I did with DWU. We went to protest in front of the house of this employer. That was a really powerful thing to me." "Do you remember what they were protesting for at that time?" I inquired. Meva responded: "Pat did not get paid what she deserved after she had received bad treatment." She was referring to another protest in support of Pat's legal case, similar to the one I attended on Valentine's Day. Protestors chanted and a DWU member delivered a speech about the ongoing case against the employer. Meva recalled:

> For me that was a powerful day. We were fighting for the rights of this lady. She was taking care of that girl like it was her kid. She worked fifty hours a week. We are fighting for her to be treated like a human being. Also, I feel like it's powerful for me because coming from Guatemala you cannot express yourself. They can kill you. To feel here safe and secure to do that kind of stuff is powerful.

Meva's impression of this protest vividly illustrates that standing up for another domestic worker emboldens those who participate. Fighting for justice on behalf of someone else—as Meva says, "for this woman to be treated like a human being"—is powerful. It demonstrates the collective power of DWU and their allies. As Meva explains, fighting on behalf of another person can also reaffirm that freedom of speech in the United States is protected; doing so together can reaffirm the right to assemble. When DWU organizes on behalf of individual domestic workers, DWU members prove to other workers that they are not alone, and their protests signal that the organization will be there to support other workers in the same way if the need arises.

During a training session on the Domestic Workers' Bill of Rights, DWU's executive director explained some of the new protections to which domestic workers would be entitled. If an employer broke the law, withheld pay, or failed to meet new legal standards or remedy an illegal situation, "We'll roll out," she declared. For seasoned DWU members, like Meva, who *have* "rolled out" across the city, the state, and the country for domestic workers' dignity and respect, this declaration reinforced what they routinely witnessed firsthand. Through their collective approach to justice through shared meals, informal conversations among members, street protests, strategizing sessions, and educational meetings, Domestic Workers United both instilled and demonstrated a vision of solidarity that offered a powerful counterbalance to the insidious racist abuse and harassment that individual workers faced in their private workplaces, illustrating to me that the real value of DWU's effectiveness in passing new laws, rallying their allies, and pursuing legal cases against abusive employers lies in its efficacy in building solidarity and power among domestic workers.

Conclusion

This story of Domestic Workers United illustrates how solidarity can be enacted among workers who are often dispersed and isolated in their workplaces, and how that solidarity can empower them. The Domestic Workers' Bill of Rights, as DWU members and their allies contend, corrects a historic wrong. And, for many individual workers and employers, the bill promises more formalized working conditions and equitable work experiences. These gains, however, come at a time of unprecedented income inequality and instability for the women and families with whom I worked. These bill's advances are meaningful but incomplete, and for many women and their families, inadequate. Yet, as we have seen, the solidarity that domestic workers have exhibited, along with their allies across industries, provides a powerful and hopeful blueprint for the future.

Their meeting spaces and protest actions demonstrate the power of solidarity beyond the important legal win of the 2010 Domestic Workers' Bill of Rights. Through camaraderie and strategizing during meetings and trainings, DWU members enacted solidarity while also instructing one another in how to improve their daily working conditions. These instances of commiseration and instruction were critically useful as working conditions for most care workers did not drastically change overnight. The passage of the Domestic Workers'

Bill of Rights itself didn't instantly improve salaries, reduce working hours, limit job duties, or resolve unpaid overtime. But the discussions, debates, and advice given during meetings and events helped DWU members support one another by sharing their own on-the-job experiences, negotiation tactics, and linguistic strategies. By contrast, many of the unaffiliated care workers I interviewed did not speak of being empowered in terms of job duties, hours, and wages. Furthermore, those outside of DWU often had not even heard about the passage of the Domestic Workers' Bill of Rights and its potential ramifications for their workplaces.

DWU's members immigrated to the United States from multiple postcolonial countries, which influences DWU's multiracial and multiethnic coalitional strategies and organizing campaigns. DWU is novel in that it strives to unite Caribbean, Latina, and African domestic workers, suggesting the organizational opportunities occasioned by globalization and its related forms of encounter and exchange. Tackling not only the labor laws from which household labor has been excluded but the individual employment dynamics inside the private homes where they work, DWU members sought to remake the care work sector through multiple avenues. As anthropologist Jane Collins (2006) argues, largely migrant, often female workers take on both employers and the state in addressing the multifaceted constraints on organizing to improve working conditions in casual sectors—like the domestic work sector. The DWU members I spoke with simultaneously critiqued features of neoliberal globalization that have robbed them of their "right to stay home" (Bacon 2013) and lauded DWU's political potential engendered by the same historical and economic forces. They saw both sides of the same globalized coin, how the histories of colonization and slavery and neoliberal policies manifest in their personal histories, workplace strategies, and political organizations.

DWU activism also enacted an incredibly effective community unionism approach in reaching out to and recruiting a broad coalition of allies to fight alongside domestic workers for the bill's passage and to inform the public of its provisions after it became law. DWU's alliances with workers in other fields, domestic workers' employers, and state legislators—so vividly illustrated by DWU members' descriptions of busloads of clergy, workers, college students, and employers of domestic workers arriving in Albany to lobby state officials—proved instrumental in passing the Domestic Workers' Bill of Rights. These alliances demonstrate the power of a diverse working class when people join together to protect one another's interests.

Narrative and affective strategies, like those used during DWU meetings, Care Congresses, and Shalom Bayit campaign events, drew an array of allies to DWU's coalition. By framing domestic work's exclusion from labor law as a historical injustice and aligning themselves with other workers excluded from labor legislation, such as farm workers, DWU's coalitional tactics reinforced ethical, religious, and political values to convince legislators in the State Assembly to champion the Domestic Workers' Bill of Rights as well.

DWU's solidarity activism successfully changed decades of labor law exclusions, yet to me the power of their solidarity is even more evident in DWU members' willingness to fight alongside one another to seek justice in individual cases of abuse, harassment, and wage theft. Their activism indicates that, despite often working alone in private homes, domestic workers can engender a sense of collective belonging through meetings, educational trainings, performances, narrative, and direct protest actions that they engage in together. Even when courts do not decide in favor of individual workers, DWU's willingness to hold abusive employers publicly accountable communicates to workers across industries that there is power in solidarity—dispelling resignation and defeat through public displays of power and unity.

Solidarity & Care offers a first-hand account of domestic workers' historic effort to pass the first labor laws covering domestic workers in the country. I have tried to recreate the process of domestic workers coming together to envision and pass the Domestic Workers' Bill of Rights, and their efforts to ensure its implementation, as an ethnographic case study, foregrounding the insights and practices that may be applicable in other dispersed industries. This ethnographic account thus also sketches a model for solidarity activism that may be transferable to the growing ranks of temporary and gig workers across industries. DWU's legislative success and continued solidarity efforts after the bill's passage provide a powerful example of how workers can overcome isolation, legal exclusions, and job instability. DWU's legacy is one of optimism, seen in a resurgence of formal labor union organizing in the United States in the wake of the COVID-19 pandemic. Service-sector employees, from coffee baristas to shipping workers employed by behemoths like Amazon, secured union victories in 2022—indicating a remarkable turning of the tides for labor union organizing in the United States.

DWU draws on and politicizes history to clearly frame care work's contributions to society. Through slogans such as "respect the work that makes all other work possible," DWU highlights the domestic labor and reproductive labor undergirding work in the productive sector. This reality—which became tragically evident during the COVID-19 pandemic—allows DWU activists to connect with working parents, adult children caring for their own parents, as well as myriad workers balancing home and work. By linking the value of reproductive labor to the political, economic, racial, and gendered aspects of domestic work, DWU uses political education to motivate workers beyond an individualistic understanding of their own particular employment and life circumstances to place their working lives in a longer historical trajectory, as well as in a broader political landscape. This educational piece proved critical in galvanizing so many diverse workers to fight for the Domestic Workers' Bill of Rights and to continue advocating for its effective implementation in private homes.

Workers across industries and activists in related social movements have much to learn from DWU, an organization of women working in private homes for low wages who successfully fought in solidarity to bring dignity and recognition to domestic work. DWU drew on radical histories of working women, mostly women of color, to ground their fight to bring dignity and respect to care work. With the passage of the Domestic Workers Bill of Rights in 2010, DWU made history. And, in their continuing fight to ensure respect for the work that makes all other work possible, they are clearing the path for future workers and activists. When I spoke with Helen about the state of domestic worker organizing recently, she told me, "It's the same way with slavery, and the same way with racism and segregation: someone set the path for us to have these conversations in an easier way. That's what we're doing with domestic work today, setting up paths so that twenty years from now, workers can just do this work and do it knowing that this is real, dignified work."

Epilogue

Solidarity in Times of Crisis

November 2020 marked the ten-year anniversary of the implementation of the Domestic Workers' Bill of Rights in New York. It was also DWU's "birthday," as the organization's email blast and Facebook page reminded me. Yet, despite these auspicious anniversaries, for many, 2020 was a year of turmoil, grief, and worry. It is difficult to convey the devastating, compounded effects of a rampant and poorly addressed global pandemic, its attendant economic crisis, housing and food insecurity, and the militarized response to protests against police brutality in African American communities, specifically the violent suppression of antiracist uprisings condemning the police killings of George Floyd and Breonna Taylor, and the attempted murder of Jacob Blake.

Domestic workers are frontline workers at the "epicenter" of these overlapping crises (Institute for Policy Studies and National Domestic Workers Alliance [IPS and NDWA] 2020). In this moment, Christina Sharpe's (2018) definition of care as "shared risk" could not be more salient. While nurses and doctors have been justifiably venerated for their efforts during the pandemic, especially early on, domestic workers infrequently received the same appreciation for or recognition of their essential labor. Many domestic workers have even remarked that the moniker "essential workers"—which applies to all of the reproductive labor positions that keep the country going day in and day out, from home healthcare workers and poultry plant workers to grocery clerks and farm laborers—would more accurately be termed "expendable workers" because of state, federal, and corporate disregard for the health, wellbeing, and safety of workers in these sectors.

Indeed, on-the-job exposure to COVID was a common hazard facing care workers. A collaboration of organizations representing domestic workers and other essential workers across the country conducted a survey in the summer of 2020 to better understand how the COVID crisis affected Black immigrant domestic workers in particular (IPS and NDWA 2020). Employers of domestic workers overwhelmingly failed to provide face coverings or recommended protective gear that might have mitigated the risk of COVID infection; 75 percent of domestic workers surveyed lacked access to personal protective equipment (IPS and NDWA 2020). Likewise, journalist Maurizio Guerrero (2020) interviewed Brooklyn domestic workers and also notes that many employers refused to don face masks in their homes, potentially exposing domestic workers to COVID.

While nurses or certified nursing assistants inside hospitals and nursing homes had to work without necessary protection, those working in private homes, like home health aides, nannies, and housekeepers, either lost their jobs entirely or experienced significantly reduced work hours. That same 2020 survey found that domestic workers in New York faced loss of income and termination in astoundingly high numbers when the pandemic began (IPS and NDWA 2020). In New York, 62 percent of the domestic workers surveyed reported that they "either lost their jobs or have fewer hours and less pay" (IPS and NDWA 2020, n.p.). Guerrero (2020, n.p.) similarly reported, "With work even more precarious than before, [domestic workers were] forced to accept lower wages." Wages fell from "$13 or $14 hour before COVID hit" to $10 dollars per hour in some cases, "even though," as one domestic worker explained, "our job is tough and considered essential" (Guerrero 2020, n.p.).

Declining wages and worsening unemployment have inevitably led to increased housing and food insecurity for domestic workers. More than half of survey respondents reported being at risk "of eviction or having their utilities shut off in the next three months" (IPS and NDWA 2020, n.p.). Similarly, anthropologist Sarah Bronwen Horton (2021, 98) writes that housecleaners and hotel cleaning staff, unable to shelter in place due to their essential labor roles, "daily faced a choice between the possibility of exposing herself at work and remaining at home only to face possible eviction."

Moreover, undocumented domestic workers were unable to benefit from the meager relief provided through the Coronavirus Aid, Relief, and Economic Security (CARES) Act (Horton 2021). Horton (2021, 100) has written extensively about how "the White House deliberately excluded from stimulus payments not only taxpaying undocumented immigrants but all citizen children and spouses listed on their taxes," characterizing this as an especially inhumane decision during a deadly pandemic. Additionally, many (43 percent) migrant domestic workers, even those with legal authorization to live and work in the U.S., reported not seeking government assistance during the early wave of the pandemic due to fear of punitive immigration enforcement (IPS and NDWA 2020).

DWU members began holding virtual town halls to communicate with domestic workers amid the pandemic. Their March 2020 town hall featured two physicians who answered questions about the virus and its spread. The next town hall covered the New York City sheltering-in-place laws, which applied to many domestic workers because domestic workers were only considered essential if they were caring for an elderly adult or for children whose parents are themselves part of an essential workforce. As a result of sheltering-in-place laws and resulting job loss, DWU members' unemployment levels skyrocketed. Accordingly, the next town hall that DWU organized covered tenants' rights and rent forgiveness. DWU also began a "love offering" campaign to raise money for unemployed domestic workers. DWU distributed these funds "to help with groceries, phone bills, and medication costs," as their email announcement explained. They also created a mask brigade to sew and distribute face coverings to domestic workers and others "in their network." DWU's activist leaders also began partnering with a community garden to deliver fresh fruits and vegetables to food-insecure domestic workers. In fact, as I was completing this book project, I often called DWU members with questions—disrupting them as they packed and distributed boxes of produce across Brooklyn.

All of these efforts evidence how critical DWU is as a source information, support, and camaraderie for New York domestic workers. It unfortunately also demonstrates how precarious care work jobs remain, and how common the experience of precarity and risk is across industries. Yet, organizers also understand this moment as an unprecedented opportunity. As the global community recognizes its shared vulnerability and as those in the United States demonstrate their care for one another through the shared risk of standing up against inhumane policing and immigration policies that target African American and immigrant communities, they animate the politics on which DWU was founded and for which its leaders still fight.

Notes

Introduction

1. The majority of the women whom I interviewed were Caribbean women who spoke English. DWU provided translation equipment to facilitate conversations in English and in Spanish at events, meetings, and rallies. I do not speak Spanish and relied on translation equipment to take notes during these bilingual events. When I interviewed women whose first language was Spanish, we spoke in English.

2. I have omitted longer discussion of feminist critiques of solidarity (hooks 1986; Mohanty 2003) and conceptualizations of neo-solidarity (Ulasowski 1998) in favor of an admittedly more romantic and perhaps superficial definition of this concept here. Elsewhere in the book, I address some of the divisions and critiques of this concept.

3. My dissertation research also encompassed participant-observation among West African women working as home health aides in New York City. For that reason, I was studying Wolof from Aminata, with whom I also developed a close friendship and from whose advice I benefitted greatly.

4. I use the term *vulnerable* in this instance with many reservations. Sociologists Shireen Ally (2009) and Jennifer Fish (2017) have astutely argued that the construction of domestic workers—and other workers—as vulnerable renders these individuals as victims and positions the government or nonprofit organizations as paternalistic saviors or protectors. Nonetheless, I did observe women workers who were vulnerable to economic exploitation and government policy as well as racist violence.

5. One final note about how I chose to write this book: Throughout, I use phrasing like "as we saw," and "as we might expect," using the first person plural noun "we" (rather than the first person singular, "I," or even a more formal approach eschewing first person pronouns). Linguistic anthropologists have noted that use of first person plural (we) "connotes a higher degree of intimacy and solidarity," which is my aim in writing this book—to draw us all into intimate solidarity with care workers and the activists of DWU (Cameron 2001, 132).

Chapter 1

1. I participated in training and data collection for this survey as part of Domestic Workers United. The study's authors—Linda Burnham and Nik Theodore—drew on 2005–2009 American Community Survey data from the United States census to ensure the study was representative of its national sample.

2. In Chapter 5, I describe how DWU responded when one of their group members' employers verbally and physically assaulted her. In this chapter, I call attention to the prevalence of this type of treatment in the domestic work sector to contextualize some of the more mundane and minor issues that also occur as a result of the isolation of these positions.

3. Many domestic workers find employment through agencies like Pamela did. But others locate employment through sites like Care.com or online parenting groups that provide nanny referrals. Many home healthcare workers and certified nursing assistants are placed in their first jobs by the training programs they attend. Still others find work through their own social networks, which can be a positive side benefit of DWU membership—hearing about job openings through other members. However, DWU's staff and board members were adamant that the organization is not a labor brokerage group and does not exist to help domestic workers find employment.

4. There are of course other factors, such as immigration status, that limit workers' negotiating power. But, in other industries, workers can join together to lessen the impact of such factors and to assert their collective rights.

Chapter 2

1. A parent cleaning, dressing, and feeding their offspring does not earn any profits through those activities. If a family hires a private chef to prepare meals in their home, the chef may earn a wage—payment for labor—but not make a profit, since their wages are not surplus. By contrast, if the private chef worked for a staffing company that accumulated profits, they would be engaged in both productive and reproductive labor, because the staffing company would capture the difference between what they paid the chef in wages and what they charged the customer as surplus or profit.

2. We could ask this question about other societies around the world, as well. And we'd come up with similar but distinct answers depending on the

region, time, and cultural beliefs. In this short chapter, I narrow the scope to the United States.

Chapter 3

1. The OECD is an intergovernmental economic organization with thirty-eight member countries, founded in 1961 to stimulate economic progress and world trade.

2. Since the 1970s, U.S. workers have not only experienced wage stagnation, they've lost significant nonwage benefits, such as employer-provided health insurance and retirement programs. The United States has also seen an increase in temporary, gig-style employment that doesn't provide overtime pay or even offer a standard work schedule while rigidly controlling workers' tasks through app-based algorithms and monitoring programs (Hua and Ray 2021).

Chapter 5

1. Brown (2011, 82) has argued that food provides a way to bring people together and create social spaces. Similarly, pathbreaking labor organizer Chris Smalls described how meals played a crucial role in building solidarity for his historic success in unionizing Staten Island's Amazon warehouse: "We had over 20 barbecues, giving out food every single week, every single day, whether it was pizza, chicken, pasta, home-cooked. . . . We did whatever it took to connect with those workers to make their daily lives just a little bit easier, a little bit less stressful" (quoted in Betts, Jaffe, and Lerman 2022).

2. These perceptions accord with Cati Coe's (2019, 6) account of African home care workers' bitterness and resignation in response to being denied political belonging and personhood in the United States.

3. I learned about the rally from close friends I made within DWU and the Shalom Bayit campaign, many of whom are linked to other activist networks throughout the tristate area and participate in a number of protests that are not directly planned by DWU.

4. Anthropologist Jemima Pierre (2004, 142) observes that characterizing someone based only on national origin or immigration status can "deny the continued significance of race and racism and the special position of 'blackness' in this country [the United States]."

Bibliography

ACLU. n.d. "How Do Labor Laws Apply to Immigrants?" *American Civil Liberties Union*. Accessed March 1, 2022. Available at https://www.aclu.org/other/how-do-labor-laws-apply-immigrants.

Adams, Kathleen M., and Sara Dickey, eds. 2000. *Home and Hegemony: Domestic Service and Identity Politics in South and Southeast Asia*. Ann Arbor: University of Michigan Press.

Adovasio, James, Olga Soffer, and Jake Page. 2007. *The Invisible Sex: Uncovering the True Role of Women in Prehistory*. New York: Smithsonian Press/Collins.

Agha, Asif. 2005. "Voice, Footing, Enregisterment." *Journal of Linguistic Anthropology* 15, no. 1 (June): 38–59.

Ahmed, Sara. 2017. "A Complaint Biography." *Feminist Killjoys* [blog]. August 9. Available at https://feministkilljoys.com/.

Allen, Theodore W. 1997. *The Invention of the White Race*. Vol. 2. London: Verso.

Ally, Shireen. 2009. *From Servants to Workers: South African Domestic Workers and the Democratic State*. Ithaca, NY: ILR Press.

Anderson, Bridget. 2000. *Doing the Dirty Work? The Global Politics of Domestic Labour*. New York: Zed Books.

Aulino, Felicity. 2014. "What's Affect Got to Do with It? Moral Labor and the Concealments of Care." Paper presented at the Society for Cultural Anthropology Meeting, Detroit, MI, May 10.

Bacon, David. 2013. *The Right to Stay Home: How US Policy Drives Mexican Migration*. Boston: Beacon Press.

Bakan, Abigail B., and Daiva K. Stasiulis, eds. 1997. *Not One of the Family: Foreign Domestic Workers in Canada*. Toronto: University of Toronto Press.

Baker, Dean. 2020. "Correction: This Is What Minimum Wage Would Be If It Kept Pace with Productivity." *Center for Economic and Policy Research (CEPR)*, January 21. Available at https://cepr.net/this-is-what-minimum-wage-would-be-if-it-kept-pace-with-productivity/.

Barnard, Anne, Adam Nossiter, and Kirk Semple. 2011. "From Hut in Africa to the Glare of a High-Profile Assault Case." *New York Times*, June 15, New York print edition, A-1.

Bayertz, Kurt. 1999. "Four Uses of 'Solidarity.'" In *Solidarity: Philosophical Studies in Contemporary Culture*. Vol. 5, edited by Kurt Bayertz. Dordrecht: Springer.

Bennhold, Katrin. 2013. "The Price of Equality." *New York Times*, October 4. Available at http://www.nytimes.com/2013/10/06/books/review/alisonwolfs-xx-factor.html.

Betts, Anna, Greg Jaffe, and Rachel Lerman. 2022. "Meet Chris Smalls, the Man Who Organized Amazon Workers in New York." *Washington Post*, April 1. Available at https://www.washingtonpost.com/technology/2022/04/01/chris-smalls-amazon-union/.

Bivens, Josh, Andrew Fieldhouse, and Heidi Shierholz. 2013. "From Free-Fall to Stagnation: Five Years after the Start of the Great Recession, Extraordinary Policy Measures Are Still Needed, but Are Not Forthcoming." *Economic Policy Institute*, February 14. Available at https://www.epi.org/publication/bp355-five-years-after-start-of-great-recession/.

Bookman, Ann, and Sandra Morgen, eds. 1988. *Women and the Politics of Empowerment*. Philadelphia: Temple University Press.

Boris, Eileen, and Jennifer Klein. 2008. "Labor on the Home Front: Unionizing Home-Based Care Workers." *New Labor Forum* 17, no. 2 (Summer): 32–41.

———. 2012. *Caring for America: Home Health Workers in the Shadow of the Welfare State*. New York: Oxford University Press.

Boris, Eileen, and Premilla Nadasen. 2008. "Domestic Workers Organize!" *WorkingUSA: Journal of Labor and Society* 11, no. 4 (December): 413–43. Available at https://doi.org/10.1111/j.1743-4580.2008.00217.x.

Boris, Eileen, and Rhacel Salazar Parreñas. 2010. *Intimate Labors: Cultures, Technologies, and the Politics of Care*. Stanford, CA: Stanford University Press.

Bourdieu, Pierre. 1998. *Acts of Resistance: Against the New Myths of Our Time*. Cambridge: Polity Press.

Braverman, Harry. 1974. *Labor and Monopoly Capital: The Degradation of Work in the Twentieth Century*. New York: Monthly Review Press.

Briggs, Charles L. 1996. *Disorderly Discourse: Narrative, Conflict, and Inequality*. New York: Oxford University Press.

Brodkin, Karen. 1988. *Caring by the Hour: Women, Work, and Organizing at Duke Medical Center*. Urbana: University of Illinois.

Brown, Tamara Mose. 2011. *Raising Brooklyn: Nannies, Childcare, and Caribbeans Creating Community*. New York: New York University Press.

Brown, Wendy, and Janet Halley, eds. 2002. *Left Legalism/Left Critique*. Durham, NC: Duke University Press.

Buch, Elana D. 2013. "Senses of Care: Embodying Inequality and Sustaining Personhood in the Home Care of Older Adults in Chicago." *American Ethnologist* 40, no. 4 (November): 637–50.

———. 2015. "Anthropology of Aging and Care." *Annual Review of Anthropology* 44 (October): 277–93.

Buchbinder, Mara. 2010. "Giving an Account of One's Pain in the Anthropological Interview." *Culture, Medicine, and Psychiatry* 34, no. 1 (December): 108–31. Available at https://doi.org/10.1007/s11013-009-9162-2.

Burnham, Linda, and Nik Theodore. 2012. *Home Economics: The Invisible and Unregulated World of Domestic Work*. New York: National Domestic Workers Alliance (NDWA).

Cameron, Deborah. 2001. *Working with Spoken Discourse*. London: SAGE.

Campbell, Stephen. 2017. *U.S. Home Care Workers: Key Facts*. New York: Paraprofessional Healthcare Institute.

Caring Across Generations. n.d. Home page. Accessed March 2012. Available at caringacross.org.

Carr, Summerson. 2009. "Anticipating and Inhabiting Institutional Identities." *American Ethnologist* 36, no. 2 (April): 317–36.

Chaney, Elsa, Mary Garcia Castro, and Margo L. Smith. 1989. *Muchachas No More: Household Workers in Latin America and the Caribbean*. Philadelphia: Temple University Press.

Chang, Grace. 2000. *Disposable Domestics: Immigrant Women Workers in the Global Economy*. Cambridge, MA: South End Press.

Chin, Christine. 1998. *In Service and Servitude: Foreign Domestic Workers and the Malaysian "Modernity" Project*. New York: Columbia University Press.

Chua, Jocelyn. 2012. "The Register of 'Complaint': Psychiatric Diagnosis and the Discourse of Grievance in the South Indian Mental Health Encounter." *Medical Anthropology Quarterly* 26, no. 2 (June): 221–40.

Clark, Gracia. 2002. "Market Association Leaders' Strategic Use of Language and Narrative in Market Disputes and Negotiations in Kumasi, Ghana." *Africa Today* 49, no. 1 (Spring): 43–58.

Coble, Alana Erickson. 2006. *Cleaning Up: The Transformation of Domestic Service in Twentieth Century New York*. New York: Routledge Press.

Coe, Cati. 2019. *The New American Servitude: Political Belonging among African Immigrant Home Care Workers*. New York: NYU Press.

Colen, Shellee. 1986. "With Respect and Feelings: Voices of West Indian Child Care and Domestic Workers in New York City." In *All American Women: Lines That Divide, Ties That Bind*, edited by Johnnetta B. Cole, 46–70. New York: Free Press.

———. 1989. "Just a Little Respect: West Indian Domestic Workers in New York City." In *Muchachas No More: Household Workers in Latin America and the Caribbean*, edited by Elsa M. Chaney and Mary Garcia Castro, 171–94. Philadelphia: Temple University Press.

Collins, Jane. 1990. "Unwaged Labor in Comparative Perspective: Recent Theories and Unanswered Questions." In *Work without Wages: Comparative Studies of Domestic Labor and Self-Employment*, edited by Jane Collins and Martha Gimenez, 3–24. Albany: State University of New York Press.

———. 2014. "What/Where Is the Working Class?" Paper presented at the Mellon Humanities Without Walls Symposium: Global Work and Working-Class Community in the Midwest, Northwestern University, Evanston, IL, September 28.

Constable, Nicole. 1997. *Maid to Order: Stories of Filipina Workers*. Ithaca, NY: Cornell University Press.

Cox, Aimee Meredith. 2015. *Shapeshifters: Black Girls and the Choreography of Citizenship*. Durham, NC: Duke University Press.

Cox, Rosie. 2006. *The Servant Problem: Domestic Employment in a Global Economy*. London: I. B. Tauris.

Cranford, Cynthia. 2020. *Home Care Fault Lines: Understanding Tensions and Creating Alliances*. Ithaca, NY: Cornell University Press.

Cranford, Cynthia, and Jennifer Jihye Chun. 2017. "Immigrant Women and Home-Based Elder Care in Oakland, California's Chinatown." In *Gender, Migration, and the Work of Care: A Multi-Scalar Approach to the Pacific Rim*, edited by Sonya Michel and Ito Peng, 41–66. London: Palgrave Macmillan.

Crenshaw, Kimberlé Williams. 1992. "Race, Gender, and Sexual Harassment." *Southern California Law Review* 65, no. 3 (March): 1467–76.

Croegaert, Ana. 2020. *Bosnian Refugees in Chicago: Gender, Performance, and Post-War Economies*. Washington, DC: Lexington Books.

Dalla Costa, Mariarosa, and Selma James. 1972. *The Power of Women and the Subversion of Community*. Bristol, U.K.: Facing Wall Press.

Damayan Migrant Workers Association. 2011. "Baklas NYC: End Labor Trafficking & Modern-Day Slavery." Accessed September 10, 2011. Available at https://www.damayanmigrants.org/baklas-nyc.

Davis, Alyssa, and Lawrence Mishel. 2014. "CEO Pay Continues to Rise as Typical Workers Are Paid Less." *Economic Policy Institute*, June 12. Available at https://www.epi.org/publication/ceo-pay-continues-to-rise/.

Dean, Jodi. 1996. *Solidarity of Strangers: Feminism after Identity Politics*. Berkeley: University of California Press.

Desilver, Drew. 2018. "For Most U.S. Workers, Real Wages Have Barely Budged in Decades." *Pew Research Center*, August 7. Available at https://www.pewresearch.org/fact-tank/2018/08/07/for-most-us-workers-real-wages-have-barely-budged-for-decades/.

Diamond, Timothy. 1992. *Making Gray Gold: Narratives of Nursing Home Care*. Chicago: University of Chicago Press.

di Leonardo, Micaela. 1991. "Gender, Culture, and Political Economy." In *Gen-

der at the Crossroads of Knowledge: Feminist Anthropology in the Postmodern Era, edited by Micaela di Leonardo, 1–50. Berkeley: University of California Press.

———. 1998. *Exotics at Home: Anthropologies, Others, and American Modernity.* Chicago: University of Chicago Press.

———. 2008. "Introduction: New Global and American Landscapes of Inequality." In *New Landscapes of Inequality: Neoliberalism and the Erosion of Democracy in America*, edited by Jane Collins, Micaela Di Leonardo, and Brett Williams, 3–20. Santa Fe, NM: School for Advanced Research.

Dill, Bonnie Thornton. 1994. *Across the Boundaries of Race and Class: An Exploration of Work and Family among Black Female Domestic Servants.* New York: Garland Publishing.

Dixon, Rebecca. 2021. "From Excluded to Essential: Tracing the Racist Exclusion of Farmworkers, Domestic Workers, and Tipped Workers from the Fair Labor Standards Act." Hearing before the U.S. House of Representatives Education and Labor Committee, Workforce Protections Subcommittee, May 3. New York: National Employment Law Project. Available at https://dedlabor.house.gov/imo/media/doc/DixonRebeccaTestimony050321.pdf.

Domestic Workers United. n.d. *Domestic Workers United.* Accessed February 10, 2009. Available at https://www.domesticworkersunited.org.

Domestic Workers United and DataCenter. 2006. *Home Is Where the Work Is: Inside New York's Domestic Work Industry.* New York: Domestic Workers United and DataCenter. Available at https://www.datacenter.org/reports/homeiswheretheworkis.pdf.

Donovan, Liz, and Muriel Alarcón. 2021. "Long Hours, Low Pay, and a Booming Industry." *New York Times*, September 25 (Updated November 1, 2021). Available at https://www.nytimes.com/2021/09/25/business/home-health-aides-industry.html.

Dudden, Faye E. 1983. *Serving Women: Household Service in Nineteenth-Century America.* Middletown, CT: Wesleyan University Press.

Duffy, Mignon. 2007. "Doing the Dirty Work: Gender, Race, and Reproductive Labor in Historical Perspective." *Gender and Society* 21, no. 3 (June): 313–36. Available at https://doi.org/10.1177/0891243207300764.

———. 2011. *Making Care Count: A Century of Gender, Race, and Paid Care Work.* New Brunswick, NJ: Rutgers University Press.

Durrani, Mariam. 2018. "#MeToo, Believing Survivors, and Cooperative Digital Communication." *Anthropology News* 59, no. 6 (November/December): e226–9. Available at https://doi.org/10.1111/AN.1062.

Ehrenreich, Barbara. 2011. "The Nannies' Norma Rae." *New York Times Style Magazine*, April 26. Available at https://archive.nytimes.com/tmagazine.blogs.nytimes.com/2011/04/26/the-nannies-norma-rae/.

Ehrenreich, Barbara, and Arlie Russell Hochschild. 2004. *Global Woman: Nannies, Maids, and Sex Workers in the New Economy.* New York: Metropolitan Books.

England, Paula. 2005. "Emerging Theories of Care Work." *Annual Review of Sociology* 31, no. 1 (August): 381–99.

Enloe, Cynthia H. 1989. *Bananas, Beaches and Bases: Making Feminist Sense of International Politics*. London: Pandora Press.

Estioko-Griffin, Agnes A. 1986. "Daughters of the Forest." *Natural History* 95: 36–43.

Farnham, Alan. 2013. "Boom Predicted for At-Home Care Industry." *ABC News* [online], April 23. Available at https://abcnews.go.com/Business/boom-pre dicted-home-care-industry/story?id=19015511.

Fine, Janice. 2000. "Community Unionism in Baltimore and Stamford: Beyond the Politics of Particularism." *WorkingUSA* 4, no. 3 (Winter): 59–85.

Fish, Jennifer. 2017. *Domestic Workers of the World Unite! A Global Movement for Dignity and Rights*. New York: New York University Press.

Foresman, Chris. 2010. "PR Firm Settles with FTC over Alleged App Store Astro-turfing." *Ars Technica*, August 27. Available at https://arstechnica.com/tech -policy/2010/08/pr-firm-settles-with-ftc-over-alleged-app-store-astroturfing/.

Fox, Justin. 2017. "The Jobs Most Segregated by Gender and Race." *Bloomberg View*, August 16. Available at https://www.bloomberg.com/opinion/articles /2017-08-1/the-jobs-most-segregated-by-gender-and-race.

Fraser, Nancy. 2016. "Contradictions of Capital and Care." *New Left Review* 100 (July/August): 99–117. Available at https://newleftreview.org/issues/ii100 /articles/nancy-fraser-contradictions-of-capital-and-care.

Friedan, Betty. 1963. *The Feminine Mystique*. New York: Norton.

Geertz, Clifford. 1973. *The Interpretation of Cultures*. New York: Basic Books.

Gerstel, Naomi, and Sally Gallagher. 1994. "Caring for Kith and Kin: Gender, Employment, and the Privatization of Care." *Social Problems* 41, no. 4 (November): 519–39.

Getman, Julius G., Stephen B. Goldberg, and Jeanne B. Herman. 1976. *Union Representation Elections: Law and Reality*. New York: Russell Sage Foundation.

Gilens, Martin, and Benjamin I. Page. 2014. "Testing Theories of American Politics: Elites, Interest Groups, and Average Citizens." *Perspectives on Politics* 12, no. 3 (September): 564–81.

Gimenez, Martha. 1990. "The Dialectics of Waged and Unwaged Work: Waged Work, Domestic Labor, and Household Survival in the United States." In *Work without Wages: Comparative Studies of Domestic Labor and Self Employment*, edited by Jane Collins and Martha Gimenez, 25–46. Albany: State University of New York Press.

Glaser, Alana Lee. 2019. "Rationalized Aging: Creative Destruction and the Subdivision of US Eldercare." *Medicine Anthropology Theory* 6, no. 2: 79–92. Available at https://doi.org/10.17157/mat.6.2.723.

Glenn, Evelyn Nakano. 1992. "From Servitude to Service Work: Historical Continuities in the Racial Division of Paid Reproductive Labor." *Signs* 18, no. 1 (October): 1–43.

———. 2012. *Forced to Care: Coercion and Caregiving in America*. Cambridge, MA: Harvard University Press.

Gomberg-Muñoz, Ruth. 2012. "Inequality in a 'Postracial' Era: Race, Immigration, and Criminalization of Low-Wage Labor." *Du Bois Review: Social Science Research on Race* 9, no. 2 (December): 339–53.

Goodwin, Jeff, James M. Jasper, and Francesca Polletta. 2001. "Introduction: Why Emotions Matter." In *Passionate Politics: Emotions and Social Movements*, edited by Jeff Goodwin, James M. Jasper, and Francesca Polletta, 1–24. Chicago: University of Chicago Press.

Grant, Roy, Delaney Gracy, Grifin Goldsmith, Alan Shapiro, and Irwin E. Redlener. 2013. "Twenty-Five Years of Child and Family Homelessness: Where Are We Now?" *American Journal of Public Health* 103, no. S2 (December): e1–10. Available at https://doi.org/10.2105/ajph.2013.301618.

Greenhouse, Carol J. 2008. "Life Stories, Law's Stories: Subjectivity and Responsibility in the Politicization of the Discourse of 'Identity'." *Political and Legal Anthropology Review* 31, no. 1 (May): 79–95.

Guerrero, Maurizio. 2020. "A Direct Legacy of Slavery, Domestic Worker Exploitation Is on the Rise in the U.S." *In These Times*, August 26. Available at https://inthesetimes.com/article/domestic-worker-labor-covid-slavery.

Harrison, Faye. 1991. *Decolonizing Anthropology: Moving Further toward an Anthropology for Liberation*. 1st ed. Arlington, VA: American Anthropological Association.

———. 1995. "The Persistent Power of Race in the Cultural and Political Economy of Racism." *Annual Review of Anthropology* 24, no. 1 (October): 47–74.

Harvey, David. 1990. *The Condition of Postmodernity: An Enquiry into the Origins of Cultural Change*. Oxford: Blackwell Publishing.

———. 2000. *Spaces of Hope*. Berkeley: University of California Press.

———. 2003. *The New Imperialism*. Oxford: Oxford University Press.

Hewlett, Barry S. 1993. *Intimate Fathers: The Nature and Context of Aka Pygmy Paternal Infant Care*. Ann Arbor: University of Michigan Press.

Hochschild, Arlie Russell. 1983. *The Managed Heart: Commercialization of Human Feeling*. Berkeley: University of California Press.

Hondagneu-Sotelo, Pierrette. 1994. "Regulating the Unregulated: Domestic Workers' Social Networks." *Social Problems* 41, no. 1 (February): 50–64.

———. 2001. *Domestica: Immigrant Workers Cleaning and Caring in the Shadows of Affluence*. Berkeley: University of California Press.

hooks, b. 1986. "Sisterhood: Political Solidarity between Women." *Feminist Review* 23, no. 1: 125–38. Available at https://doi.org/10.2307/1394725.

Horton, Sarah Bronwen. 2021. "On Pandemic Privilege: Reflections on a 'Home-Bound Pandemic Ethnography.'" *Journal for the Anthropology of North America* 24, no. 2: 98–107. Available at https://doi.org/10.1002/nad.12150.

Howell, David R., and Arne L. Kalleberg. 2019. "Declining Job Quality in the United States: Explanations and Evidence." *Journal of the Social Sciences* 5, no. 4 (September): 1–53. Available at https://doi.org/10.7758/RSF.2019.5.4.01.

Hua, Julietta, and Kasturi Bhadra Ray. 2021. *Spent behind the Wheel: Drivers' Labor in the Uber Economy.* Minneapolis: University of Minnesota Press.

Ibarra, Maria de la Luz. 2013. "Frontline Activists: Mexicana Care Workers, Subjectivity, and the Defense of the Elderly." *Medical Anthropology Quarterly* 27, no. 3 (September): 434–52.

———. 2016. "The Ties that Bind: Mexicana Caretakers and Aging Americans Construct Kinship." *Anthropology of Work Review* 37, no. 2 (November): 79–90. Available at https://doi.org/10.1111/awr.12099.

International Labour Organization. 2015. "ILO Warns of Widespread Insecurity in the Global Labour Market." *International Labour Organization, Newsroom.* May 19. Available at https://www.ilo.org/global/about-the-ilo/newsroom/news/WCMS_368252/.

IPS and NDWA. n.d. *Notes from the Storm: Black Immigrant Domestic Workers in the Time of COVID-19.* Institute for Policy Studies and National Domestic Workers Alliance. Available at https://www.domesticworkers.org/wp-content/uploads/2021/06/IPS-WDiB-survey-brief-English.pdf.

Jasper, James. 2011. "Emotions and Social Movements: Twenty Years of Theory and Research." *Annual Review of Sociology* 37: 285–303.

JFREJ. n.d. "Our History." *Jews for Racial and Economic Justice.* https://www.jfrej.org/our-history.

Jimeno, Myriam. 2007. "Cuerpo Personal y Cuerpo Colitico: Violencia, Cultura y Ciudadanía Neoliberal." *Universitas Humanísticas* 63 (January–June): 15–34.

Jones, Jacqueline. 1985. *Labor of Love, Labor of Sorrow: Black Women, Work, and the Family, from Slavery to the Present.* New York: Basic Books.

Katznelson, Ira. 2013. *Fear Itself: The New Deal and the Origins of Our Time.* New York: Liveright Norton.

Kilgannon, Corey. 2007. "Long Island Couple Convicted of Enslaving 2 Domestic Workers for Years." *New York Times,* December 18, 2007. Available at https://www.nytimes.com/2007/12/18/nyregion/18slave.html.

Kleinman, Arthur. 2009. "Caregiving: The Odyssey of Becoming More Human." *Lancet* 373, no. 9660 (January): 292–93.

Kugelmann, Robert. 1999. "Complaining about Chronic Pain." *Social Science and Medicine* 49, no. 12 (December): 1663–76.

Lan, Pei-Chia. 2006. *Global Cinderellas: Migrant Domestics and Newly Rich Employers in Taiwan.* Durham, NC: Duke University Press.

Laslett, Barbara, and Johanna Brenner. 1989. "Gender and Social Reproduction: Historical Perspectives." *Annual Review of Sociology* 15 (August): 381–404.

Lasser, Carol. 1987. "The Domestic Balance of Power: Relations between Mistress and Maid in Nineteenth-Century New England." *Labor History* 28, no. 1 (January): 5–22.

Linde, Charlotte. 1987. "Explanatory Systems in Oral Life Stories." In *Cultural Models in Language and Thought,* edited by Dorothy C. Holland and Naomi Quinn, 343–66. Cambridge: Cambridge University Press.

Longmire, Linda, and Lisa Merrill, eds. 1998. *Untying the Tongue: Gender, Power, and the Word*. Westport, CT: Greenwood Press.

Lopez, Steven. 2014. "Culture Change and Shit Work." *American Behavioral Scientist* 58, no. 3 (September): 435–52.

Mabrouki, Abdel, and Thomas Lebègue. 2004. *Génération Précaire*. Paris: Le Cherche Midi.

Macdonald, Cameron Lynne. 2010. *Shadow Mothers: Nannies, Au Pairs, and the Micropolitics of Mothering*. Berkeley: University of California Press.

Macleod, Morna, and Natalia De Marinis. 2018. *Resisting Violence: Emotional Communities in Latin America*. London: Palgrave MacMillan.

Madison, D. Soyini. 2010. *Acts of Activism: Human Rights as Radical Performance*. Cambridge: Cambridge University Press.

Marx, Karl. (1932) 1961. *Economic and Philosophic Manuscripts of 1844*. Moscow: Foreign Languages Pub. House.

———. (1867) 1977. *Capital*. Volume One. New York: Vintage Books.

Masi de Casanova, Erynn. 2013. "Embodied Inequality: The Experience of Domestic Work in Urban Ecuador." *Gender and Society* 27, no. 4 (April): 561–85.

Matthews, Cara. 2010. "Domestic Workers Get Labor Protections under New Law." *Democrat and Chronicle*, August 31. Available at https://www.democratand chronicle.com/story/news/politics/blogs/vote-up/2010/08/31/domestic-work ers-get-labor-protections-under-new-law/2171075/.

McGranahan, Carole. 2016. "Theorizing Refusal: An Introduction." *Cultural Anthropology* 31, no. 3 (August): 315–25.

Mead, Margaret. 1935. *Sex and Temperament in Three Primitive Societies*. New York: William Morrow.

Melosh, Barbara. 1982. *The Physician's Hand: Work Culture and Conflict in American Nursing*. Philadelphia: Temple University Press.

Melville, Juliet A. 2022. "The Impact of Structural Adjustment on the Poor." Paper prepared for the Eastern Caribbean Central Bank Seventh Annual Development Conference, Basseterre, St. Kitts and Nevis, November 21–22.

Milkman, Ruth. 1987. *Gender at Work: The Dynamics of Job Segregation by Sex during World War II*. Urbana: University of Illinois Press.

———. 2012. "Immigrants and the Road to Power." *Dissent* 59, no. 3 (Summer): 52–57.

Milkman, Ruth, Helen Reese, and Benita Roth. 1998. "The Macrosociology of Paid Domestic Labor." *Work and Occupations* 25, no. 4 (November): 483–510.

Millar, Kathleen. 2014. "The Precarious Present: Wageless Labor and Disrupted Life in Rio de Janeiro, Brazil." *Cultural Anthropology* 29, no. 1: 32–53. Available at https://doi.org/10.14506/ca29.1.04.

Mills, Mary Beth. 2005. "From Nimble Fingers to Raised Fists: Women and Labor Activism in Globalizing Thailand." *Signs: Journal of Women in Culture and Society* 31, no. 1 (September): 117–44.

Moghari, Shaghayegh. 2020. "Representation of Angel-in-the-House in *Bleak House* by Charles Dickens." *Journal of Humanistic and Social Studies* no. 2:

47–63. Available at https://www.proquest.com/openview/2c0abe73560edf1 b0e4e40597a8cd6f8/1.

Mohanty, Chandra Talpade. 2003. *Feminism without Borders: Decolonizing Theory, Practicing Solidarity*. Durham, NC: Duke University Press.

Muhl, Charles J. 2001. "The Employment-at-Will Doctrine: Three Major Exceptions." *Monthly Labor Review* 3 (January): 3–11.

Mulla, Sameena. 2014. *The Violence of Care: Rape Victims, Forensic Nurses, and Sexual Assault Intervention*. New York: NYU Press.

Mullings, Leith. 2005. "Interrogating Racism: Toward an Antiracist Anthropology." *Annual Review of Anthropology* 34, no. 1 (October): 667–93.

Nadasen, Premilla. 2009a. "Domestic Workers Take It to the Streets." *Ms. Magazine* (Fall): 38–40.

———. 2009b. "'Tell Dem Slavery Done': Domestic Workers United and Transnational Feminism." *Scholar and Feminist Online* 8, no. 1 (December): 238–41. Available at https://doi.org/10.5406/jcivihumarigh.2.2.0238.

———. 2015a. "Domestic Workers' Rights, the Politics of Social Reproduction, and New Models of Labor Organizing." *Viewpoint Magazine* (October). Available at https://viewpointmag.com/2015/10/31/domestic-workers -rights-the-politics-of-social-reproduction-and-new-models-of-labor-or ganizing/.

———. 2015b. *Household Workers Unite: The Untold Story of African American Women Who Built a Movement*. Boston: Beacon Press.

Naiman, Robert, and Neil Watkins. 1999. *A Survey of the Impacts of IMF Structural Adjustment in Africa: Growth, Social Spending, and Debt Relief*. Washington, DC: Center for Economic and Policy Research.

Naples, Nancy A. 1998. *Grassroots Warriors: Activist Mothering, Community Work, and the War on Poverty*. New York: Routledge.

Nare, Lena. 2011. "The Moral Economy of Domestic and Care Labour: Migrant Workers in Naples, Italy." *Sociology* 45, no. 3 (June): 396–412.

National Domestic Workers Alliance. n.d. "Domestic Work Is an Engine of New York City's Economy." *National Domestic Workers Alliance*. Accessed August 15, 2022. Available at https://www.domesticworkers.org/member ship/chapters/we-dream-in-black-new-york-chapter/nyc-care-campaign /new-york-city-domestic-work-factsheet/.

New York City Department of Consumer Affairs. 2018a. *Lifting up Paid Care Work: Year One of New York City's Paid Care Division*, March. Available at https://www1.nyc.gov/assets/dca/downloads/pdf/workers/Lifting-up-Paid -Care-Work.pdf.

———. 2018b. *Workers' Bill of Rights: New Amendments to NYC's Paid Safe and Sick Leave Law*, June. Available at https://www.nyc.gov/site/dca/workers /workersrights/know-your-worker-rights.page.

Ngai, Mae M. 2004. *Impossible Subjects: Illegal Aliens and the Making of Modern America*. Princeton, NJ: Princeton University Press.

Noah, Timothy. 2013. *The Great Divergence: America's Growing Inequality Crisis and What We Can Do about It*. Princeton, NJ: Princeton University Press.

Oakley, Ann. 1972. *Sex, Gender and Society*. London: Temple Smith.

Ochs, Elinor, and Lisa Capps. 1996. "Narrating the Self." *Annual Review of Anthropology* 25, no. 1 (October): 19–43.

Omi, Michael, and Howard Winant. (1986) 2015. *Racial Formation in the United States*. 3rd ed. New York: Routledge.

Ong, Aihwa. 1991. "The Gender and Labor Politics of Postmodernity." *Annual Review of Anthropology* 20, no. 1 (October): 279–309.

Orloff, Ann Shola. 1993. "Gender and the Social Rights of Citizenship: The Comparative Analysis of Gender Relations and Welfare States." *American Sociological Review* 58, no. 3 (June): 303–28.

Ortner, Sherry B. 2019. "Practicing Engaged Anthropology." *Anthropology of This Century* 25 (May). Available at http://aotcpress.com/articles/practicing-engaged-anthropology/.

Ostry, Jonathan D., Prakash Loungani, and Davide Furceri. 2016. "Neoliberalism Oversold?" *Finance and Development* 53, no. 2 (June): 38–41.

Ozyegin, Gul. 2001. *Untidy Gender: Domestic Service in Turkey*. Philadelphia: Temple University Press.

Palmer, Phyllis. 1989. *Domesticity and Dirt: Housewives and Domestic Servants in the United States, 1920–1945*. Philadelphia: Temple University Press.

Paquette, Danielle. 2017. "The Fastest-Growing Jobs in America Pay about $22,000 a Year." *Washington Post*, November 12. Available at https://www.latimes.com/business/la-fi-healthcare-jobs-20171113-story.html.

Parish, Anja. 2017. "Gender-Based Violence against Women: Both Cause for Migration and Risk along the Journey." *Migration Policy Institute*, September 7. Available at https://www.migrationpolicy.org/article/gender-based-violence-against-women-both-cause-migration-and-risk-along-journey.

Parreñas, Rhacel Salazar. 2001. *Servants of Globalization*. Stanford, CA: Stanford University Press.

———. 2005. "Long Distance Intimacy: Class, Gender and Intergenerational Relations between Mothers and Children in Filipino Transnational Families." *Global Networks* 5, no. 4 (October): 317–36.

———. 2008. *The Force of Domesticity: Filipina Migrants and Globalization*. New York: New York University Press.

Partis, Michael. 2019. "The Making of Racial Caste in Post-Truth America." *American Anthropologist* 121, no. 1 (February): 170–72.

Perea, Juan F. 2011. "The Echoes of Slavery: Recognizing the Racist Origins of the Agricultural and Domestic Worker Exclusion from the National Labor Relations Act, 72 OHIO ST. L.J. 1 95 (2011)." Ph.D. diss., Loyola University Chicago. Available at https://lawecommons.luc.edu/cgi/viewcontent.cgi?article=1150&context=facpubs.

Pierre, Jemima. 2004. "Black Immigrants in the U. S. and the 'Cultural Narratives' of Ethnicity." *Identities: Global Studies in Culture and Power* 11, no. 2 (April): 141–70.

Pine, Adrienne. 2013. "Revolution as a Care Plan: Ethnography, Nursing and Somatic Solidarity in Honduras." *Social Science and Medicine* 99: 143–52. Available at https://doi.org/10.1016/j.socscimed.2013.05.028.

Poo, Ai-jen. 2010. "Organizing with Love: Lessons from the New York Domestic Workers Bill of Rights Campaign." *New Left Turn*, December 1. Available at https://www.leftturn.org/Organizing-with-Love.

———. 2011. "A Twenty-First Century Organizing Model: Lessons from the New York Domestic Workers Bill of Rights Campaign." *New Labor Forum* 20, no. 1 (February): 50–55.

Povinelli, Elizabeth A. 2002. *The Cunning of Recognition: Indigenous Alterities.* Durham, NC: Duke University Press.

Price, Richard. 2011. *Rainforest Warriors: Human Rights on Trial.* Philadelphia: University of Pennsylvania Press.

Reed, Touré F. 2020. *Toward Freedom: The Case against Race Reductionism.* London: Verso.

Reese, Ashanté. 2019. "Refusal as Care." *Anthropology News* 60, no. 3 (May/June). Available at https://doi.org/10.1111/an.1181.

Rollins, Judith. 1985. *Between Women: Domestics and Their Employers.* Philadelphia: Temple University Press.

Romero, Mary. 1992. *Maid in the U.S.A.* New York: Routledge.

Rosaldo, Michelle Zimbalist, and Louise Lamphere, eds. 1974. *Women, Culture, and Society.* Stanford, CA: Stanford University Press.

Said, Edward. 1978. *Orientalism.* New York: Vintage Books.

Sarti, Raffaella. 1999. *Globalization and Its Discontents: Essays on the New Mobility of People and Money.* New York: New Press.

———. 2016. "Historians, Social Scientists, Servants, and Domestic Workers: Fifty Years of Research on Domestic and Care Work." *International Review of Social History* 59, no. 2 (July): 279–314.

Sassen, Saskia. 1991. *The Global City: New York, London, Tokyo.* Princeton, NJ: Princeton University.

Scelfo, Julie. 2008. "Trickledown Downsizing." *New York Times*, December 10. Available at https://www.nytimes.com/2008/12/11/garden/11domestics.html.

Schnitzler, Antina von. 2014. "Performing Dignity: Human Rights, Citizenship, and the Techno-Politics of Law in South Africa." *American Ethnologist* 41, no. 2 (April): 336–50.

Scott, James. 1985. *Weapons of the Weak: Everyday Forms of Peasant Resistance.* New Haven, CT: Yale University Press.

Sen, Indrani. 2008. *Memsahib's Writings: Colonial Narratives on Indian Women.* Hyderabad: Orient Longman.

Shambaugh, Jay, and Ryan Nunn. 2017. "Why Wages Aren't Growing in America."

Harvard Business Review, October 24. Available at https://hbr.org/2017/10/why-wages-arent-growing-in-america.

Sharpe, Christina. 2018. "And to Survive." *Small Axe: A Caribbean Journal of Criticism* 22, no. 3 (November): 171–80.

Shaw, Jennifer, and Darren Byler. 2016. "Precarity." *Cultural Anthropology.* Accessed January 1, 2021. Available at https://journal.culanth.org/index.php/ca/catalog/category/precarity.

Shermer, Elizabeth Tandy. 2018. "The Right to Work Really Means the Right to Work for Less: Why Business Interests Have Spent 70+ Years Crusading for Right-to-Work Laws." *Washington Post,* April 24. Available at https://www.washingtonpost.com/news/made-by-history/wp/2018/04/24/the-right-to-work-really-means-the-right-to-work-for-less/.

Shiffrin, Nancy. 1987. *What She Could Not Name.* La Jolla, CA: La Jolla Poets.

Simpson, Audra. 2017. "The Ruse of Consent and the Anatomy of 'Refusal': Cases from Indigenous North America and Australia." *Postcolonial Studies* 20, no. 1 (January): 18–33. Available at https://doi.org/10.1080/1368879 0.2017.1334283.

Smedley, Audrey. 2007a. "The History of the Idea of Race . . . And Why It Matters." Presented at the conference Race, Human Variation and Disease: Consensus and Frontiers, sponsored by the American Anthropological Association (AAA). March 14–17. Available at https://www.communitysolu tionsva.org/files/History_of_the_Idea_of_Race_-Audrey_smedley.pdf.

Smedley, Audrey. 2007b. *Race in North America: Origin and Evolution of a Worldview.* Boulder, CO: Westview Press.

Smith, Joshua. 2009. *American Jobs Plan: A Five Point Plan to Stem the American Jobs Crisis.* Washington, DC: Economic Policy Institute. Available at https://www.epi.org/publication/american_jobs_plan/.

Smith, Rebecca, Ana Avendaño, and Julie Martínez Ortega. 2009. *Iced Out: How Immigration Enforcement Has Interfered with Workers' Rights.* Washington, DC: AFL-CIO. Available at https://ecommons.cornell.edu/bitstream/han dle/1813/88125/afl_cio16_IcedOut_report.pdf?sequence=1&isAllowed=y.

Sparr, Pamela, ed. 1994. *Mortgaging Women's Lives: Feminist Critiques of Structural Adjustment.* Chicago: University of Chicago Press.

Stacey, Clare L. 2011. *The Caring Self: The Work Experiences of Home Care Aides.* Ithaca, NY: ILR Press.

Sullivan, Paul. 2015. "Finding a Nanny Who Fits with Your Family." *New York Times,* January 23. Available at https://www.nytimes.com/2015/01/24/your -money/finding-a-nanny-who-fits-with-your-family.html.

Susser, Ida. 2010. "The Anthropologist as Social Critic: Working toward a More Engaged Anthropology." *Current Anthropology* 51, no. S2 (October): S227–33. Available at https://doi.org/10.1086/653127.

Sutherland, Daniel. 1981. *Americans and Their Servants.* Baton Rouge: Louisiana State University Press.

Sztandara, Magdalena. 2021. "'We Are Fed Up . . . Being Research Objects!' Negotiating Identities and Solidarities in Militant Ethnography." *Human Affairs* 31, no. 3: 262–75. Available at https://philpapers.org/rec/SZTWAF.

Tattersall, Amanda. 2008. "Coalitions and Community Unionism: Using the Term Community to Explore Effective Union-Community Collaboration." *Journal of Organizational Change Management* 21, no. 4: 415–32. Available at https://doi.org/10.1108/09534810810884821.

Taylor, Diana. 2003. *The Archive and the Repertoire: Performing Cultural Memory in the Americas*. Durham, NC: Duke University Press.

Train, Rob. 2022. "How Many Paid Vacation Days Do Workers in Other Countries Get?" *Diario AS*, June 20. Available at https://en.as.com/latest_news/how-many-paid-vacation-days-do-workers-in-other-countries-get-n/.

Twigg, Julia. 2000. *Bathing: The Body and Community Care*. New York: Routledge.

Ulasowski, Nina. 1998. "'It's a Hard Row to Hoe, Girl': Feminist Solidarity in Women's Antiwar Activism: Women in Black and the Dilemma of Difference." Honors thesis, University of Queensland. Available at http://www.gilasvirsky.com/femsolidarity.html.

Vitello, Paul. 2007. "Couple Held Two Servants Captive for Years, U.S. Says." *New York Times*, May 16. Available at https://www.nytimes.com/2007/05/16/nyregion/16slave.html.

Weil, David. 2017. *The Fissured Workplace: Why Work Became So Bad for So Many and What Can Be Done to Improve It*. Boston: Harvard University Press.

Wolfe, Julia, Jori Kandra, Lora Engdahl, and Heidi Shierholz. 2020. "Domestic Workers Chartbook: A Comprehensive Look at the Demographics, Wages, Benefits, and Poverty Rates of the Professionals Who Care for Our Family Members and Clean Our Homes." *Economic Policy Institute*, May 14. Available at https://www.epi.org/publication/domestic-workers-chartbook-a-comprehensive-look-at-the-demographics-wages-benefits-and-poverty-rates-of-the-professionals-who-care-for-our-family-members-and-clean-our-homes/.

Zavella, Patricia. 1991. "Reflections on Diversity among Chicanas." *Frontiers: A Journal of Women's Studies* 12, no. 2: 73–85.

Index

ALANA LEE GLASER is Assistant Professor of Anthropology at St. John's University.

www.ingramcontent.com/pod-product-compliance
Lightning Source LLC
Chambersburg PA
CBHW071349280326
41927CB00040B/2558